The Folds *of* *Insurgency*

Attention Authors

Manas Publications is fighting a war to tell the world that India can win the battle not only by bullet but also by pen. We are converting fighters into writers as there is no dearth of intellectuals in our country but their knowledge is confined to them only. No sincere effort has been made by any other publisher to give right direction to their knowledge and the talent of every intellectual is lying hidden. An author always gives the raw material in the shape of a manuscript and it depends on a publisher how to make it a finished product. We are motivating the intellectuals' mind and publishing their manuscripts for more than two decades and would like to publish your manuscript, too. If you or your colleagues have any manuscript or are working on it, please don't hesitate to contact us with detailed synopsis and contents, for its publication. We take utmost care in production and give wide publicity to the book and its author. We can also suggest you the title related to your subject for writing, as we are the publishers who believe more in quality than in quantity.

The Folds *of* Insurgency

A.P. Maheshwari, IPS

Foreword by

Prakash Singh, IPS (Retd.)

Manas Publications
New Delhi-110002 (INDIA)

MANAS PUBLICATIONS
(We Convert Fighters into Writers)
(Publishers, Library Suppliers, Importers & Exporters).
4402/5-A, Ansari Road (Opp. HDFC Bank)
Darya Ganj, New Delhi-110 002 (India)
Off. (23260783, 23265523 Fax: 011-23272766
E-mail: manaspublications@vsnl.com
manaspublications@gmail.com

2nd Impression 2012 (FP – 2008)

ISBN 978-81-7049-331-0
₹ 495/-

Designed at
Manas Publications

Printed in India at
Harmain Offsets, Delhi
and published by Mrs Suman Lata for
Manas Publications, 4402/5-A, Ansari Road
(Opp. HDFC Bank), Darya Ganj,
New Delhi-110 002 (INDIA)

Dedicated to all those who have been the victims of violence emanating from the Insurgencies (of life)

DISCLAIMER

All the names and characters are fictitious and any resemblance with the reality would be merely coincidental. This is also not a true depiction of any historical fact of the area. Nothing in this publication amounts to an official stand on any matter, what so ever.

FOREWORD

The north-eastern India has been a turbulent theatre of conflicts. There are ethnic groups seeking assertion of their identity by demanding recognition. There are tribal groups seeking autonomy or even secession. The region has been convulsed by conflicts ever since the mid-fifties, when Phizo raised the banner of revolt in the Naga Hills. The prairie fire soon spread to Mizoram and thence to Manipur and Tripura. Assam witnessed disturbances in the eighties over the illegal migration of Bangladeshis into the State, giving rise to an apprehension in the minds of the Assamese, that they would be overwhelmed by the sea of humanity flooding their territory. The situation was exploited by the United Liberation Front of Assam (ULFA), which harped on the alleged economic exploitation of the State by the Centre, to demand freedom from the Indian "colonial regime."

The multi-layered conflicts in the region forced the government to undertake armed action against the separatist and insurgent outfits. There were allegations and counter-allegations. The rebels accused the government of committing excesses and violating human rights. The government blamed the militant outfits of stirring up trouble, killing innocent people, blowing up railway tracks, kidnapping people for ransom and disturbing peace in the area.

Conflict situations, especially those which drag over a long period of time, produce all kinds of aberrations. The rules of the game or laws of war are all thrown to the winds and the uppermost consideration is to achieve the political objective – of autonomy or independence by the insurgent outfit and their defeat and subjugation by the government. In the process, the finer human instincts get blunted.

The author has, in this remarkable book dwelt at length on deviant behaviour, distorted attitudes and questionable practices witnessed in a society torn asunder between demands for separation or secession on the one hand and the paramount consideration of upholding national integrity on the other. The 'Silhouette' is a painful story of Debojit, a police officer, and his wife, Charu separating over their differing political convictions. Debojit is eventually killed by the insurgents in a striking parallel to the annihilation of DS Negi, Superintendent of Police, by the ULFA rebels. The circumstances of killing in the 'Silhouette' are however poignant with Charu herself partaking in the elimination of her own husband.

The 'Fragments' are a collection of stories which bring out the sinister aspects of counter-insurgency operations. Gopang, who had joined the insurgents but was subsequently retracing his steps and was keen to join the mainstream, was disposed off by the police which was keen to show results after they had suffered reverses. The fact, that Gopang was the only earning member of his family did not bother the men in uniform. The stories make us think about the futility of such conflicts and the heartlessness that goes into actions from both the sides.

Maheshwari has been very candid in his portrayal of what happens below the surface in conflict situations – the intrigues, the conspiracies, the shortcut methods which have no sanction under the law, the special operations which are an euphemism for statistical results achieved by dubious methods, the CATs nurtured by the law enforcement agencies who tend to become a law unto themselves, the staged encounters, etc. These are based on first-hand experience during his stint in Assam, where he served as Commander of a paramilitary outfit.

The book forces us to ponder. Why can't the government concede the legitimate political aspirations of a group without creating a situation where people feel that recourse to arms is the only alternative left? Why can't the rebels pursue their political objectives through peaceful methods? Why can't the insurgent outfits and the police and the paramilitary forces ensure that the common man is not harassed and the innocents are not victimized? Why can't the differences be resolved across the negotiating table?

The tide is fortunately turning in the north-east. The premier militant outfit of Assam, the ULFA, stands discredited for having become a stooge of Pakistan's ISI.

Nagaland has had a prolonged period of peace even though the contours of a final settlement are still hazy. Manipur has a plethora of insurgent outfits, but these are currently bereft of any ideology. In Tripura, insurgency is tapering off. Meanwhile, government's Look East policy has started producing dividends. The seven states of the region are in the process of combining to form a beautiful rainbow on the north-eastern horizon. "Peace hath her victories no less renowned than war."

Prakash Singh

[Decorated with 'Padam Shree' in the year 1991 for his outstanding contribution to National Security, Shri Prakash Singh has been a distinguished officer of Indian Police Service and rose to be the Chief of UP Police in the State and also the Border Security Force in the Centre. His contribution in combating the insurgency in Nagaland and Assam, stemming the tide of terrorism in Punjab as well as tackling the militancy in Kashmir have been laudable and widely recognized.]

PREFACE

This is a modest effort to bring to the reader the varied silhouette of the life of the people living in the insurgency prone areas of Assam. Here, they somehow eke out a living, constantly torn between the pulls and the pressures of the sovereign and the subdued.

When insurgency fans out of the house, it stands witness to the ploys and manoeuvres of a horde of players, all in the game with different levels of stakes. But is there even one amongst them who can claim to be genuinely interested, even inclined to solve the problems at hand?

It is their displaced goals at varying levels that leads to deflected responses which are very rarely in conformity with the desired normative.

Yet, life must go on. The varying levels of struggle will also continue to permeate and target our lives. And, thus, the evident silhouette of the 'defacto' will not become the aspired reflections of the 'dejure'.

It is unavoidable that in the situation of a low intensity conflict management, there will emerge several sets of trade offs.

Thus, the police force, which is the visual arm of the Government manages the show very often at the cost of their own family life. The desolation, that hereby sets in their life as a consequence, very often results in abject disillusionment. Yet, they continue to function under such adverse circumstances. And, if this state of desolation is to be termed as a state of peace, there can be no greater human misfortune.

In addition to the main story 'Silhouette', here are penned down some other 'Factual Fragments' that make deep inroads into the psyche along with various aspects of the lives of the soldiers fighting the insurgency. These short stories reflect another ignored dimension of the fragmented insurgency of human emotions.

A.P. Maheshwari

A Short Preview

Part-I

SILHOUETTE

This story hovers around various facets of insurgency prevalent in the lower parts of Assam. The series of distortions emerging from the multi-layered impact of history, demography and cross-cultural confluence, notwithstanding the economic interests, get reflected in the violence that eludes all initiatives to spread peace and harmony. The undercurrents are distinctly reflective of the game plans of various stake holders. The fractured crust of emotions gradually gives way to volcanic eruptions which, in turn, create fresh modified landscapes.

Charu and Debojit, a couple, whose life starts on a note of love and affection, become victims to the long drawn insurgency. Amity gradually turns into enmity. Radical thoughts and subdued emotions lead the couple to a new plateau which is marred by undulating ravines of personal aspirations. The role and goal conflicts pull them apart. Charu takes on to insurgency which her father had nurtured years back, while Debojit, a cop, takes the insurgents head on. A story of bedroom love converts into a battlefield saga. 'All is fair in love and war', the much quoted idiom deflects all the ideals. Whether it is a family or society at large, the rules of the game appear to be the same when insurgency sets in to fracture all the intricately woven webs of relationships.

Systemic response to the problem clearly follows a set pattern. Political manoeuvering presents a naked picture of ulterior motives for personal gains. The Police is used to contain and crush the upsurge till a convenient solution emerges. The inventory of terror and brutality has high returns for all the players in the game. The economics of terrorism keeps the hidden interest of many stakeholders alive, while the visual arm of the governance i.e. the police develops its own sub-culture to survive and stage manage the show, internal devaluations notwithstanding.

The story brings out hard realities of insurgency and counter-insurgency formats, the game we may not dare to play.

Charu treacherously gets Debojit killed in the hope to win the game but her 'inner-self' induces endless tears in her eyes once he is gone. The Silhouette of human manipulation leaves us bewildered: "Would the Sun ever shine again?"

Part-II

FRAGMENTS

Added to the main story are some fragments of facts depicted by the short stories, touching different aspects of life of the soldiers fighting insurgency. This is another dimension of insurgency of fractured emotions. There are ten such stories:

- Encounter
- Operation 'CATS'
- Its Not About Guns Alone
- All Part of the Game
- Special Operations
- Charred Bamboos
- Suicide
- Shoot out
- The Incentive
- Reflections of a Cop

CONTENTS

Part-II: Fragments

Part–I

Silhouette

Chapter One

THE ECHO

Her heart beat rose vehemently in revolt. Revolting against the lurking, unknown threat!

Charu Basumetary, sitting on the banks of the river Brahmaputra was lost, deep in thought. An intense echo of protest was gradually building in her but had frustratingly failed to pierce through the bewildering, deep, thicket of bamboo groves surrounding her. The fast dying rays of the fading sun were skillfully playing tricks with the churning waters of the Brahmaputra forcing it to change its coloured hue from a shimmering, inviting cool blue to the ominous shades of a threatening grey and black. The growing shadows of the silent trees seemed to be emerging threateningly from the interiors of the belly of the river, rearing hungrily to engulf her. She watched, burning hot with indignant rage, yet helpless to change the course of the Brahmaputra as its waters challengingly galloped under the much trodden, worn out, wooden contraption that had served as a bridge for over a decade.

It brought memories of only a few years back, of her father's words that echoed in her ears, "I am committed to the cause of the liberation force. You shall see! We shall have independent existence. We want autonomy and we shall have it. We will no longer allow this step motherly treatment to our people to continue. Very soon it shall be 'We', who will set the pace of the development in our area. Yes! You just wait and see!"

Her eyes turned moist, brimming with the unshed tears she had held back all these years. She clearly remembered those awful men in khakhi and olive green, how they had forced their entry into their modest home, a thatched hutment, mercilessly dragged her father out and whisked him away, while the mother and daughter's duo had remained mute and helpless spectators to that inhuman assault.

Her mother had slipped into a state of mute shock when after two days the news, that her father was killed in an encounter with the forces, had spread like wild fire through out their village. Charu's immature, inexperienced mind could not fathom the seriousness of the situation. Her father had been declared a militant? No, Bishon, her father was a national hero, a freedom fighter who would liberate her people from the shackles of the gross humiliating chains of injustice that had tied them down. Gradually, as the years rolled by, her mistrust for those in power grew along with a belligerent conviction that was taking firm roots in her 'she would not let her father's sacrifice go waste.'

'Bamboo', the life sustainer was gradually sucking them dry. Their seamy lives had become so complexly enmeshed within the winding, never ending rows of the branching bamboo stretches, overcast by the deep, lengthening shadows of the threatening bamboos. Their shackled freedom was gasping for a breath of fresh air. The ever spreading tentacles of its roots were gradually reducing them to a wasting barrenness that was devoid of any ray of hope. It had become a constant, pathetic struggle of survival amongst the ever-growing branches of corruption, exploitation, extortion, reducing them to an abject state of penury, distrust and hopelessness. A lesser mortal would have panicked and surrendered in this hostile environment. The angry waters of the Brahmaputra were constantly spouting venom as against the deceivingly innocent silence of the bamboo groves. But not so with Charu!! Against this heightened, unfriendly backdrop, the long brewing revolt within her kept growing interminably, till it had reached intimidating proportions. Wherein lay the difference!. Though the insurgency in their area suited them all, yet those claiming to be at the helm of the liberation front actually enjoyed an ostentatious life-style. Those aping to be 'the Messiah' had actually turned bestial – callously indulging in the exploitation of those, whom they put up an extravagant show of rescuing, but were actually condemning them to the ignominy of the flesh trade and other such unimaginable, emotional atrocities. The supposed Samaritan himself was screwing the 'common' faith to gain their selfish, personal satisfaction. The line of demarcation between the tactics of those who coveted an autonomous land in the future and the modus operandi of those hungering for political power had today become difficult to define. 'Development' now had a novel connotation-'exploitation'. The 'poor' found themselves in a hopeless situation. Their lives now reeked of the exhuming stench of the still waters and the stifling weeds. Their skeletal forms slouched further under the burden of their raped, tortured, enslaved, mutilated remains.

The moon was beginning to emerge from behind the dense, multiple layer of clouds. A few isolated stars were also faintly visible as they struggled to twinklingly register their presence amidst the dense threatening cover. The evening was beginning to get typically nippy. An unwitting shiver ran down her spine as the surroundings gradually turned further unfriendly. She realised she could not linger on there any longer. Back home, her husband, a cop, would be returning soon, expecting her to greet him at the door.

"Hi! Where have you been, darling?" Debojit Basumetary fondly queried as Charu entered her house, and then without really expecting a reply continued - "And, how was your day?"

"Just fine", mumbled Charu.

"Hey, something on your mind? Can I be of some help?" Debojit carried on his playful banter, tweaking her pretty little stubborn nose as he approached her.

"I am not amused! Won't you ever learn when to lay off! I know you are looking pleased as punch. Its no hidden secret that you are enjoying every moment of being a part of the very system I have picked up cudgels against, a system that is slowly and surely gnawing away at the very roots of my people. And you, you had taken the oath to stay by my side through thick and thin. Yet, look at you today. I sometimes wonder, do I really know you? Did I ever for that matter?" Charu's pent up fury finally found release.

"There, we are back again to the same, pointless badgering. Will it ever enter your thick head, my sweet,

sweet sweetheart that you are my world, and would I hurt my own world? I am not so unfeeling, nor so stupid, you know! We are united for not just the present but for eternity, my ridiculous doll! You won't get rid off me so easily".

Charu gave him a cold, distasteful look before turning away.

"Why must it always come back to the same old issue with you? I have borne it long enough; I will not stand it any more. You will not see me as someone separate from you. I honour your sentiments and respect you all the more for the same... I love you my dear and you shall always find me beside you, willing to lay down my life for you. Hey, still want to take my breath away," Debojit's playful humouring was rudely interrupted by Charu's retort, "Don't think even for a fraction of a second that I will be misled by all these cajoling tactics of yours. I've long been wise to them. Its despicable how you guys will go to any length to prevent us from posing a potential threat to the 'establishment'."

"You know, that's not true! You infact are the more fortunate, being in a position to air your grievances, while we here are unable to do even that. Our lips are sealed by the dictates of the government we serve".

"Government? Ha! What government? You mean that satanical, deceitful farce that claims to be our benefactor. And the whole lot of you, you are all just touts of that ruling party."

"There you go again. Don't pass such sweeping judgment. You know deep down in your heart that it does not hold true for me. Yes, I accept that I have on some counts taken strong measures against those that have flouted the law, but then, if I were not to do so, I would be dishonest to my profession. Would you wish I was unprofessional in my approach?"

"You know, that I am still with you 'cause I respect your honesty to your commitment, else we would have gone our separate ways long back."

"So then! Where lies the problem? Come, lets forget all our differences and retreat into our world where my enchanting wife dotes on her henpecked dodo of a husband, a husband who comes back to her, hoping to be offered the mellowing warmth of her love, to be encircled by her welcoming arms that take him away from and make him forget all the day's ugliness and its rewardless grind", an overwhelmed Debojit pulled her close. Momentary relief swept over her and assuringly wrapping her shapely arms around his well toned neck she lifted her face up, to welcome his anxious expectant lips. Just then, time came to a stand still as they held each other tightly, each attempting to draw comforting sustenance from the other. Those frustrating years, where they had been mere frustrated mute spectators, were washed away in the endless sea of love. The sense of intense bitterness that had transformed this bubbly, vivacious chit of a girl into a bitter, pensive pessimist had for the time being taken a back seat. Instead, here was a woman soaked in the engulfing passion of love and flushed with the intense desire for a man she had long cherished.

How long they remained in each others welcoming arms and when Charu slipped into a deep peaceful slumber, her anguished frail frame eventually succumbing to the much needed rest was difficult to determine.

She was alone again when the vibrant musical chimes of the old grandma's clock in the adjoining living room woke her up. Her eyes flitted to the dial of her wrist watch, it was just about past midnight. Debojit was nowhere to be seen, but it did not come as a surprise to her. Over the years she had become used to waking up in the wee hours of the night to find her husband missing from her bed – probably out for the night patrolling or laying an ambush, or may be carrying out a fake encounter, torture, confession. The list just got more and more gory and gruesome. Sometimes she failed to identify with this side of him, this cold, heartless, calculating individual. Was this butcher, this insensitive contract killer of the government, her sensitive, gentle caressing and capable lover in bed. There also lay between them a long history of heated arguments. They had made several futile attempts to convince each other, "What is the difference between you and the contract killers people hire to kill. You go on a killing spree every time those in power instruct you to do so! Don't you have a conscience any more? When will you ever realise that these medals that supposedly adorn your chest and that you exhibit with immense pride are actually literally soaked in the blood of the innocent as well?"

Suddenly overwhelmed with intense exhaustion and feeling totally sapped of energy, Charu realised she had skipped both the major meals of the day. Her stomach was in a rebellious mood. She could hear it rumbling hard in protest. She got up to sit at a lonely table that was otherwise meant to seat four. Despite the years of sitting alone to eat at the table at most meal hours, she still missed 'his' presence. She distractedly nibbled slowly at the frugal serving on her plate. Inspite of the extreme difference of opinion between them she still loved the man she had first fallen so deeply in love with. She could feel him deeply entrenched within her system. But over the years, it had gradually grown into an unexplainable love-hate relationship, where despite abhorring him intensely she still yearned for his proximity.

Shaking off her depression and willing herself to prevent wallowing in self pity, she prepared to go back to sleep realising she needed a good nights sleep to be able to face what lay ahead on the coming day.

Tomorrow was going to be one of those difficult days. She would be leading a group of activists to mark a strong protest against the violation of human rights – the molestations, the killings and the torturing of both the young and the old. She made a mental note of the slogans and the points of reference for her speech, the dialogue she intended to deliver before the Divisional Commissioner.

She was still lost in the jigsaw puzzle of oration, those powerful, invoking and moving words when she heard the siren of a jeep approaching the driveway to the house. Then followed the familiar purposeful foot steps and she got up from her bed to open the door for her waiting husband at the entrance.

☆ ☆ ☆

Chapter 2

THE FOOTSTEPS

The echoing sound of the approaching foot steps resounding in the silence of the night always sent Charu several years back to her childhood when her father would often return home late, long after most of the dark hours had slipped away. Yet, his announcing, purposeful stride would shake her out of her deep sleep. She would then lazily pull herself out of the circle of her mother's unresisting arms into the reassuring lap of her father. He would then gently pick her up and pat her off to sleep as she snuggled up in the warmth of his bed, encircled within the assurance of his ample arms. His gentle dealings never failed to surprise her. A demi-god, so strong, revered by the entire clan with so many mind boggling heroic tales circulating around him, this vulnerable side of his personality had overwhelmed her with a growing, deep rooted respect for him.

The initially baffled poppet had soon become aware through hearsay about her father's involvement in some movement that would liberate her people from both the clutches of misery and the poverty that had long been the scourge of their lives. Yet, she was not able to appreciate the ethnocentric views of the elders in the clan. However, as she had matured in years, the ethnic differentiations gradually began to penetrate across a frozen perceptual background.

The sound of footsteps gradually grew distinct, till they halted for a fleeting second and then resumed again as he pushed open the door that had been left ajar by Charu. She had unbolted it, knowing instinctively that it would be Debojit.

Debojit entered the room and directed a furtive glance towards Charu's face in order to assess the reception he would get today. Finding her in reasonable humour his posture unwittingly relaxed, "Still awake, my dear! Sometimes I do wish I had an ordinary 'nine to five' desk job. Why do you stay up for me, dearest? Go get some beauty sleep, I shall be beside you within seconds, just allow me a few seconds to get into something more comfortable."

Softly humming a few nostalgic lines of the song they had often sung together in those adolescent years when they had first met across their college canteen table and finally fallen in love, Debojit entered the bedroom. His eyes fell upon the half open folder with its papers sprawled in total disarray all over his side of their double bed.

"Now, now, what mischief has my good for nothing darling been up to! Whatever it be, shall have to wait. His majesty, your spouse is tired and needs to curl up and sleep in her majesty's comforting arms and certainly not amidst this bundle of disconcerting overwhelming sermons!" quipped Debojit. The long years of togetherness had taught Charu all the necessary tactics of tackling her hubby, "You've always been my rock of Gibraltar you know, always reliable, always ready and willing to help whenever I've needed your support. I need your help once again my dear, help me prepare my speech for tomorrow, please," cajoled Charu instead.

"Any thing for you my dearest. Now what is this all about?" responded Debojit who had never been able to resist this enticingly appealing side of hers. Anxious to ensure the success of her talks the next day, Charu elaborated, "We have been pressing the authorities to withdraw the armed forces from the area. Instead, they need to take recourse to 'real' measures that would ensure the upliftment and finally put an end to the sufferings of the sons of this soil who unfortunately, so far, have found themselves completely alienated in their own homeland."

"Do you really think that things are going to be that simple? My dear, there have now surfaced many controversial and disturbing facets to the present scenario".

"What do you then suggest? Do you feel picking up the lead from a historical perspective would help resolve these issues?"

"It would make sense if we were looking for mere analysis of the situation. But I fail to see how it would help you effectively drive home your point?"

"On the contrary, it shall help to make it absolutely clear, and will clearly drive home the point I am trying to make. Don't you agree that migration has been the root cause of the whole problem? The demographic transformations that took place over a period of time are, I feel, largely due to the diverse socio-political reasons...."

"No, I wouldn't agree totally with this line. After all, later on the migrations took place predominantly due to economic reasons, you know."

"Okay, so let's figure it out stepwise. Now, who are the Bodos? We claim that we are the Bodos! But, they say, that, we are in fact the Mongoloid migrants descending from Tibet & West China. Whereas, factually, Dimasa, Bodo, Mech or Boro are the nomenclatures given to the same class in the Northern Central, Southern and Western sections of the valley."

"Okay, conceded, but then what relevance does it hold now? That was ages back. If you wish to dwell only in the past, then even the Varmanas, Melechchas and the Pala dynasties ruled here thereafter, so..."

"See, now you are coming to my point of view. It was, in fact, Prince Sukhapha of the Thai family who had come down from the Shaw area of Myanmar as long back as in the 13th century and that is how the Ahom dynasty flourished. You know by the 16th century they conquered almost all the kingdoms in and around the Brahmaputra Valley. Even Mir Jumla, the Mughal General of the Tughlaqs couldn't reach beyond Gargaon in 1662. Aurangzeb's army was eventually defeated in 1671 at Saraighat.

That is not to say that the Ahoms had it going good for them throughout. Krishna Narayan, whose father Hangsa Narayan, the ruler of Darrang, was killed by the Ahom ruler Gaurinath Singha, had vowed to take revenge. He had resolved to drive the Ahoms out of Assam. Eventually, the Ahoms did bite the dust. They were defeated by the 19th century and the Myanmaris, thereafter, ruled the roost. However, finally the Britishers managed to defeat them too and completely took over after the Anglo-Myanmar war in 1824."

"I am suitably impressed."

"No, why should you be? I am just a blockhead. Cops, after all, come minus their grey cells."

"Peace for now, darling. I am really tired and desperately need some sleep now."

"Aahah! lend me your ears for a few more minutes now that you have raised the issue, will you?"

"I'm telling you it has right through been a blatant play of exploitation. Exploitation of the ignorant labourer in the tea estates that led to the exploitation of the Nagas. The British gave away conciliatory gifts to the tribals, like enlisting them in the Army. Then, Assam as you know has huge forest reserves, vast stretches of tea plantations while the population there is comparatively sparse. The Santhals from Bihar, therefore, came in as 'cheap fillers'. Then 'the Marwaris' entered. They shrewdly sensed the trade potential, while the British imported the civil servants from the state of Bengal. Then, the Nepalese grazers also gradually filtered in. This has resulted in a predominant cellular character in an Assamese society devoid of any harmonious fusion. It, thus, provided a comfortable, inviting platform for colonial consolidation, commercial exploitation and the increasing feudal attitudes of the landlords. Those who had come in from outside the boundaries of the state now formed the cream of the society here, while the local inhabitants faced the devils of deprivation and scarcity."

"See, now that explains......."

"No, not completely. You see, the masses are still making do with the bare minimum, dwelling in crude Changhars (bamboo hut) and filling their growling bellies with Kharicha (bamboo pickle). These are the tongueless, faceless milieu that suffer in deafening silence. They hold no opinion, they exist without a presence, they make no impact; they just roll with the times. And ironically, the few lucky devils amidst them that experience some economic and political upliftment, work only at making quick personal bucks and then very conveniently disappear to luxurious, opulent abodes seeking political asylum. The poor, lost and bewildered middle rung, remained to face the brunt of this hopeless situation. So naturally, it is they who now react and revolt against these sub human living conditions."

"Yaah, we know all about their power of speech. No wonder! They still remain the puppet on a string at the complete mercy of their exploiters."

"You just don't figure it out, do you? You are just too simple darling and frightfully high strung. This emotionality shall get you nowhere but into very serious trouble. Take heed, I warn you. I know much more about this big bad world, trust me!"

"Yet, you can......."

"Hey, Ma'm! I wanna make one thing very, very clear! We, unfortunately for us, are presently stuck in a system where most people, I wouldn't say all, who advance in life eventually come to exploit it for their own gain. In principle, I completely agree with you, because even when the funds for development were there, they never got channelised into the starving fields. Instead, they were brazenly used to fill up the coffers of the already corrupt. The corrupt became more corrupt and prospered while...."

"I am happy that despite your being an integral part of the corrupt system you, at least, have the decency to acknowledge it", derided Charu.

"That's not fair. Now, that's typical middle class psyche. Without getting to the bottom of the issue you've drawn your conclusions and passed judgment simply to suit your convenience."

"Now don't you think you are pushing the issue too far. I suggest let's drop it for now!"

"That's funny, coming from you. First, you coax me into a discussion I was disinclined to indulge in, and then when I put my views before you, you feel I am just going on and on unnecessarily. God help me! It's difficult to understand what makes a woman's mind tick."

"Okay, that's enough. Thanks for coming forth with so many ideas and thus enabling me to see the issue from a completely different perspective. It has helped me to make up my mind and has given me a clear direction that my argument should take."

"No, on the contrary, I wish to thank you for finding at least something positive in what I've said. Can I, if I may be allowed, turn in now?"

"Yes, you are now permitted to do just that!" Charu indulgently ran her fingers gently through Debojit's tousled unkept hair. Debojit's head inadvertently dropped lower to find solace in the beckoning nape of her neck.

Sleepily, he mumbled, "Do I earn some 'vantage points' now?"

"Yes, you've earned them all", fondly Charu moved closer, letting her fingers intertwine between the thick curling, unruly growth on his chest.

And then, the distant sound of the running waters of the Brahmaputra intermingled with their emotional outburst as they waded into the vast, overpowering ocean of love. The clear, translucent sky, the blinking stars and the sombre moon encircled by its soothing, shimmering hue stood mute spectators to the overwhelming tide of the warm reflections of their engulfing emotions.

Spent, yet content, an hour later Charu whispered lazily into Debojit's ear, "I'll still be going ahead with the programme, haha!"

Debojit appeared tense, his brows furrowed both in concern and apparent disapproval. A few moments now hung heavy between them. Then, a sigh of resignation escaped his lips and with a helplessness writ all across his expressions he nodded, "I'd have loved to have supported you in your lofty aims, instead we have stringent orders to block your path."

"Are you expecting violence too?", a concerned Charu now heard herself asking.

"I really don't know. But God knows I wish there isn't".

They had unwittingly moved closer, holding each other for a few moments in a suffocating bind. Desperately, each wished the reality away. For that moment time stood still. And so clasped in each others arms, they fell asleep. When Charu's eyes opened, Debojit had already left for duty.

* * *

Chapter 3

THE IMPENDING TIDE

The threatening rugged terrain with its harsh, hostile topography zig-zaggedly sketched with the sinewy, winding pony tracks that cut deep furrows along the hill slopes and the sharp, dipping gorges with the angry waters snaking its path through these narrow divides, offered a daringly vivid contrast to the warm valleys reverberating with the cheerful gurgle of the Brahmaputra that gently endorsed the prevalent serene tranquility around. Interspersed with the refreshing whisper of the surrounding air, this valley projected the comforting warmth of a safe cocoon.

Here, nature at its best, offered tranquil solitude, a spiritual peace under the reassuringly transparent, blue canopy that was erratically streaked with brilliant hues of the intermixed shades of orange and red. The patiently spreading light in the far east, happily hailed the arrival of another glorious morning.

Yet, Charu was overcome with a persistent sense of restlessness. Peace eluded her. She felt sickeningly repulsed at her weak flesh and her last night's indulgences. Her head was exploding with a throbbing pain and her limbs were overcome with a strange restlessness, an exhaustion that refused to leave her.

Even her Debojit, today, seemed just another stumbling block, who had failed to do what she had expected of him. He had left, not bothering to wake her up. If only he had realised the urgency of what lay ahead of her, and the magnitude of the effect of his carelessness today. He had known all along that this meeting meant a lot to her. Years of relentless effort might finally find direction and he, of all the stupid things to do, had left her sleeping while he left for work. Oh God! They really were growing apart, fast becoming complete strangers to each other's needs. Life never did fail to spring its fair share of surprises.

She hurriedly went over the points, scribbling down a few lines on a piece of paper that she had found lying on the dining table and then stuffed it carelessly down her front purse pocket. She now made an unsuccessful attempt to restore the glow to her lifeless features with an artificial layer of the beauty aids that adorned the shelf that stood against the six feet long looking glass placed right adjacent to her bed.

Quickly gulping down a hot steaming cuppa' tea along with a couple of Marie bikies, she left.

As the invaluable seconds were ticking away, she was finding it increasingly difficult to keep up the pace. Her frantic effort to drive fast were further frustrated by the incessant potholes on the pitiable excuse of a road, which seemed like it was another continuous mute protest against the rampant corruption and the gross neglect of public convenience.

Her anxiety was growing by leaps and bounds with each fleeting second. After a fair quota of bumps and jolts, she finally arrived attempting to make a discrete entry into the function's pandal.

The vast multitude of nameless faces turned, their eager eyes following the approaching gracefully attired figure as she made her way to the dais just when her name was being announced.

As she crossed over to the dais, similar scenes fast forwarded before her eyes- familiar speeches, stage acrobatics and pointless ramblings of often repeated, unkept promises made over the years to the gullible milieu. Nothing really ever seemed to change, except for the changing sea of the expectant faces that still looked at their leaders for an eventual realisation of their ageing dreams.

They believed in us, yet, she realised, they had managed to evolve no further. This jarring truth continued to compound Charu's head as she briskly covered the steps to reach the group of her community torch bearers, the so called messiahs of the wretched who were already occupying the dais.

With these familiar outbursts still ringing in her ears unabated, another shock now awaited her.

A fresh surge of panic gripped her veins as the much dreaded face of the Chief of their Armed Wing, Arabindo Deka, came into clear focus. Almost in a trance, with bewilderment writ large all over her expressive features, she moved to occupy the vacant seat right next to him.

"What in heavens sake are you doing here? I'm afraid I fail to comprehend the need for your presence. Don't you see, your presence here today could jeopardize our mission? They are on the look out for you, you are a marked man. You are a wanted man, you know. The establishment is raring for your head, yet you have the gall to appear on this public dais today. Have you even lost the capacity to think straight any longer?" A visibly perturbed Charu, after a moment's pause, continued,

"Isn't it after all for our political wing to mobilise the masses. This is no place for you. Your presence here may only eskew the situation further. You do realise, don't you, that you are important to our cause," hissed Charu, all the while furtively glancing in all directions and added, "Making a public appearance probably in disguise would have made more sense. What the hell were you thinking of when you decided to come here anyways?"

"I really can see no cause for panic. I'm anyway leaving shortly," came a churlish retort from Deka and then carelessly pushing the issue aside he continued -

"Enough! Let us not be the judge of that. The Chief is there to decide these issues. Anyway, if the administration should resist our functioning, it may not bode well for them".

"Indeed! Now that would be truly foolish..........."

"On the contrary, you blockhead, that is exactly our intention! We want to invoke a harsh reaction from them, an onslaught........" chuckled an evil beaming Deka.

"But, what about these innocent masses, these unsuspecting women with their infants in their arms, these children, the young and the wisened old jostling in the crowds. They are here, completely unaware of this lurking danger."

"This, unfortunately, is all part of the game. It is a loss that we must bear. Some heads have to roll. This unsuspecting crowd collected here is more the reason for us to encash on this volatile situation. We will successfully invite a resistance from them by painting the present administration as the vile 'Oppressor'."

"If this has been the plan all along, then we at least deserved to be informed earlier. We should have been taken into confidence", Charu stamped her foot in indignation. Her insides were beginning to hurt........... and even if................."

Charu could feel her face growing red. She felt slighted, cheated of her beliefs. The words of resistance rising within her failed to find verbal expression as she heard her name announced repeatedly on the microphone.

She was seething with rage. Yet, she managed to compose her features enough to break into a smile. With a few quick steps she reached the microphone, warmly greeting the restive crowd. But they seemed to be no longer receptive to her charms. The wait was beginning to take its toll. Their piercing eyes seemed to beseech, 'how far and how long'.

Charu could feel their frustration slowly seeping in, tingling her bones. She felt the connection, the village scene, the barely covered scrawny frames hopelessly searching for weeds in the filthy excuse of a pond. Their eyes turned towards the distant skies, the vacant stares of helplessness flashed vividly across her mind. As she echoed these thoughts aloud from the podium, the pandal reverberated with approving claps and the shrill parched cries of the milieu. She had noticed the elaborate police arrangement in the rear sections of the gathering. They were, as if, waiting to pounce on the unsuspecting public, as it responded to rebel call. However, the enthusiasm of the rallyists despite the threatening presence of the state forces was a heartening sight. Their monstrous presence seemed not to have a daunting effect on their spirits as they rallied on in the sapping heat for endless hours.

Charu recognised the cop in command. It was Debojit. Their eyes locked for a fleeting second and then looked away. Another closer look across the crowd and she could see, it was made up of demurely clad housewives with their young ones tugging at their sarees, intermingled rows of spirited youth, with the tired yet hopeful working lot and the aged frail forms wanting and still waiting. The trusting light of expectancy still burnt bright in those otherwise lifeless, tired eyes.

But, there was also disgust writ large on all the faces that constituted this soled throng, a contempt for the intruders which was marred by Charu's agonizing cry- "Why us, we the aborigines, we are left with this hand to mouth existence while these foreign intruders, these immigrants dictate the terms and conditions of our existence, our very survival? What has driven us to feel like aliens in our own house? The insecurity of our drab existence has now forced us to become the minority while they are no longer the docile entrants, the domesticated cattle meant to do our bidding." While Charu's soul searching delivery was having the much needed effect on the crowd, generating the desired tempo and flush, she continued to remind them of the possible attempts by the power brokers, these mischief mongers to try and create a divide, to effect fissures amongst the flanks of the assiduously nurtured tribal society.

"We have our own cultural lineage. Why then do we need the dictates of these aliens?" she continued to press deeper home.

All the while, Debojit was intently lending his ear to his wife's delivery, carefully weighing her words and the extent of their damage. For, he was here on another mission. He had strict instructions from his seniors to contain the tide. He could clearly foresee the advent of a brewing storm. The tranquil air was misleading. There was molten lava struggling to erupt and pour over the quiet exteriors. Unfortunately, he was in this unhappy situation where he would face the music and their wrath as he was representing their enemy, the administration. He was well aware that his shrewd bosses were, at the moment, rubbing their palms in malicious glee as they now had the rubble in the very predicament that they had hoped for. The pronounced 'sons of the soil' flavour had a clandestine sprinkling by some opposing groups that had been sponsored by the power brokers. And Debojit was well aware that he was a mere pawn in this sweeping game plan. Yet, he was helpless. He could clearly visualise, or much rather he knew, that the bastion of the ultras was soon going to witness a pale shadow of the turbulence. The government in power had also very shrewdly begun an anti-campaign in order to carefully assess the average bend of the local clouts, that is, those that could make a difference. They mattered and were not to be nettled with.

In the meantime, some of the leaders of the ultras found themselves in an explosive situation having been exposed for their nefarious tendencies. Their recently acquired undeserving affluence - the foreign bonanza they enjoyed........the lure of easy money now had them securely in its clutches and above all, the sexual indulgences they had succumbed to, clearly boded their imminent nemesis with the power tacklers using these very chinks in their armour, to exterminate them. The trade offs, the crisscrossing was sufficient to baffle the perceptual sensors of the common man.

Intuitively sensing the brewing trouble, Charu reorganised her thoughts. She now tried to take a firm grip of the situation by making another attempt to gain control and bring back some semblance of order to the situation. "As you have repeatedly seen for yourself, nothing really matters to the well-to-do stratum of the immigrants except to control the power equations. We are the ones that sink, we are the ones weighed down with the burden of the debris of backwardness, with no possible avenues for growth, with languishing investments, with rising unemployment for our youth. Beware! Do not make the mistake of being buoyed by the speculations made by the existing government. Surreptitious propaganda will not make a dent here. We owe it to our motherland not to waver from our cause. We are on a pious mission. Our struggle for freedom shall continue unabated. Is it acceptable that a motley group who are already oppressed and suffering should suffer further gross injustice?" Then, directing her ire at the paid government servants on duty, she screamed, "Does your conscience not pinch you? How can you ignore its callings and listen instead to the selfish datum given by our power manipulators. Is your sensitivity so deadened by the lure of money and medals that you would walk over the carcasses of these already ill fated souls, this poor hapless sea of the suffering to receive your material remunerations. Don't.........." But Charu's sentence faded in mid air as a deafening blast split the sky wide open.

Hell broke lose. Before people could react, the police had come into action. Charu's eyes searched for Deka but he was nowhere to be seen. She pleaded for restraint, but her desperate cries failed to pierce their ears above the screaming uproar. She looked on haplessly, a mute spectator to the brutalities of the police. The old and the young fell alike, trampled in the stampede. The mangled shamiyana, the piercing screams, the blood dripping faces......... Charu stood stupefied in a daze. Gradually, as it all began to sink in, her entire body, shook with uncontrolled rage. Overwhelmed with despair, she pushed herself to make one last ditch effort, jumping down the dais amongst her own people. She had barely landed on her feet when a full swing brunt from a baton landed on her left temple knocking her unconscious. The attack had come from Debojit. The wild swing of the baton had failed to differentiate between the leader and the led, between a male and a female, much less a spouse. Her supporters immediately formed a human barrier to protect her from further assault. Debojit pushed through the crowd and ordered her arrest. The crowd went ballistic. The situation had lost all semblance of sanity, the mob went berserk, the miscreants amongst them set on fire whatever they could lay their hands on. As the skies turned grey with smoke, indiscriminate gunshots had a field day on unsuspecting, hapless preys. Several innocents perished that day. Absolute mayhem prevailed. The survivors ran helter skelter, desperate for refuge from the indiscriminate spray of bullets. Their noble mission was a thing of the past. The need of the hour was to reach a spot that would provide shelter from the wrath of the angry bullets, may it be found behind the make shift shop structures or under a rusted tin sheet, behind a pillar, in a sewer- any place that would keep them safe. Others seemed rooted to their spot, too shaken to move. The line of demarcation between cowardice and bravery had in that hour, lost its significance. Even time seemed to stand still, dazed at the magnitude of human vile!

Gradually, the town limped back to normalcy. The leaders were released in the evening. Back in Debojit's home, a threatening silence loomed in the air. Charu, moved around their house performing her chores as if in a trance. Debojit, unsure of how things would progress, maintained a studied silence. The unease seemed to be growing in bounding proportions between them. Unable to bear it any further, Debojit made a few unsuccessful, half hearted attempts to strike a conversation between them. His meaningless quips were received with an icy silence. Time seemed to have come to a halt.

It struck midnight. The chiming of the clock jarred the eerie silence that prevailed in the house. Turning and twisting restlessly in bed, Debojit made one last ditch effort to break the ice between them. He gradually moved and snuggled up to her, in an attempt to take her in a bear bug. Her reaction was unexpectantly violent, "You, you bastard, how dare you touch me with those filthy hands! You dare assume that I would allow you, your so called rights after the way you treated me in the pandal", screamed Charu like a restrained animal that had been finally unleashed. "Cool it Charu! Here, we are just husband and wife", Debojit persisted cajolingly.

"You fiend! You lusting bastard! Are you even remotely concerned about my emotions? Do my dreams figure anywhere in your needs? You are, after all, just like all the usual males-selfish, self centered, an egotist! You desire my body, you can have it, but you have lost me forever", Charu broke down, tears streaming down her face. Hurting emotions that had been kept under check so far now poured out unrestrained!

When she finally fell asleep, was difficult to tell. Debojit too had gone into a helpless trance staring at the moving wings of the creaking overhead fan for hours; before the needs of the tired body took over and dulled his senses into deep slumber.

Thereafter, the dark threatening night faced an uprising tide. Belligerently, the bamboo in the forest loomed larger than the rearing tide in the room. The space in the room shrank, threateningly!

* * *

Chapter 4

BREACHES IN THE BARRAGE

Bright sunlight filtered through the mosquito netted windows, filling up the master bedroom with a warm morning glow. Debojit dug his face deep into his pillow, covering it in an attempt to escape the blinding sun that intruded upon his much needed sleep. Suddenly, sensing something amiss, he leapt out of his bed, his eyes travelling to the wall clock overlooking their bed. It read 'nine'! God, where was everybody? And where was Charu? What was wrong with her? Why hadn't she woken him up earlier? Now, he was going to be late for work. Where was she? An agitated Debojit called out to her, but the only response he got was an eerie, a sinister, a threatening silence. His call echoed across the corridors of the desolate house and returned.

Frantic, he left the bed and moved through the rooms of the house calling, "Charu! Charu! Dear, where are you? I am late for work." But his words got no response. Desperation had begun to creep into his voice. O God! Where the hell had she disappeared so early in the morning? A sense of foreboding was beginning to take over. He roughly pushed aside the bedroom curtain to peep into the backyard and made one last attempt to reach out to her, "Charu, where are you? My darling, don't I get some breakfast today?" Debojit was now beginning to panic. Where could she be? She had made no mention of going anywhere? Where could she be? Where had she disappeared? And soon, the cop in him took over. He moved through the house scrutinising the rooms for any tell tale signs. As he entered the living room a sudden breeze tipped the grotesque figure of the laughing Buddha that had stood since ages on the mantelpiece facing the main entrance to the house and was shattered to pieces. O God! A bad omen! A cold shiver travelled down his spine. Something was seriously amiss.

Bewildered, he entered the master bedroom. His eyes did a quick make over, systematically progressing through the room. From the corner of his eyes he noticed a white slip of paper uncertainly peeping from under the pillow on his side of the bed. A sense of foreboding overcame him as he stretched out his hand to reach the piece of writing. With trembling hands, he unfolded the slip. Scanning through its content, he could feel himself growing cold. His entire world came crashing down. A strong sense of dizziness overcame him. His feet failed to provide support. Fumbling desperately he reached out for some concrete support. His hands brushed against the side of the reclining sofa in the far corner of the room. He stumbled, then taking its support gradually slipped into its cushioned seat gasping for air. His nostrils quivered as he gradually lost control and broke down. Curling into a foetus like position he howled like a desperate child who had lost his favourite possession forever. Tears streamed down his rough cheeks streaking the day's stubble on them. This could not be happening to him. Yes, they had had their moments of differences, but that there would ever come a time when they would part, was something that had never even fleetingly crossed his mind. How would he live without her, he did not know how to live without her, more so how could she fathom an existence without him? This was just a bad dream and he would soon wake up and realise that it was just his hideous imagination playing tricks on him. That Charu had left him forever; the words echoed and pierced his insides. He suddenly felt life completely drain out of his limbs. He had never felt so helpless, so alone and so discarded in life. Could Charu truly have the heart to do this to him. Had she turned so callous and so unfeeling! "No....don't leave me........ I will not be able to survive this agony Charu, have pity on me," screamed Debojit to the mute, unfeeling walls. He tore the chit to bits and scattered them around the room, he could feel his temples throbbing, his nerves taut, ready to burst, he gripped his head between both his palms in a desperate attempt to quieten them down. His head reeled and the room around him gradually turned a dark shade of crimson.

Her words kept ringing through his head. "Debojit, I am leaving you. This is as much as I can take. I cannot say if we shall meet again. It is not that I am not aware of all that you've done for us, for our relationship. Yet, its not enough. You've let me down. I did not get from you the support that I should have had. I feel so let down. So betrayed! You were unable to give me the unflinching support I had the right to expect from my spouse. You have been aware right from the start of the struggle that this was my life's mission. And the challenges I was ready to undertake. Yet, we ended up working at cross purposes........"

Tears filled Debojit's eyes as he repeatedly scanned through Charu's departing accusations. With each word, the incidents, the emotions raced through his mind at lightning speed. He recalled those moments, her rigidity of reaction and belief, her refusal to see sense in all his warning. Despite his constant towing to her wishes, her over assertive life style, she still looked upon him with constant disapproval. Her statement was like a blade piercing his heart, ".........You know, I never really needed a man in my life. Had it been possible for women to bear children without men, I would never have let a man into my life........". He felt demeaned, was this all that he meant to her, a means to conceive, and create a life by merely using him? He felt lost. His world was coming crashing down all around him. Each word on the dotted lines, penned in Charu's letter hit him hard again and again, "......Do not think, that you had me fooled for a moment. You have never wanted my mission to succeed from the start. You never really empathised with my cause, my needs, my wants and my ambition. All you ever wanted was an alluring female who would dance to your tune, declothe for you, play whore to your physical demands....... good that I did not conceive your child." Debojit could no longer bear the venom her words spouted.

The allegatory exposition had shaken him up. Such deep rooted hatred, so much poison had been brewing inside her against him. Had their marriage been a mere farce from day one. Were all his hopes and demands so unreasonable, so selfish, as she made it out to be. No, this was not true. This couldn't be true. He had honestly loved her, wanted only happiness for her. Whenever he had gone against her beliefs, it was not because he desired it so, but because his hands were tied, he had been duty bound. Could he wish her ill, never? He had truly cared for her, doted on her. But then how far could he have stretched his neck out for her. He would not be a traitor to his cause, that he would not do. And, if that meant being unfaithful to her, then yes, he was a selfish bastard, and he was not concerned about her! So be it. How far and how long was he expected to give in to all her whims, her self-centred demands, her self-opinionated quips without her ever bothering to show even an iota of concern for what he wanted of her, of how he felt and of what she owed to him. Was he truly the leech she had painted him out to be? She had managed to reduce him to the status of a rag picker, the constant deprivations he had suffered without ever voicing the extreme moments of loneliness, the terrible ache gnawing away at his insides......... and then her constant reminders of it being a single file march through life. And, he had accepted it all without any retaliation, any resistance. Yet, to ditch him like this....... The humiliation was becoming unbearable........"

Suddenly, the shrill chimes of the wall clock attracted his attention to the time it announced. "Oh, God, it is 10:30. I am late." His head unwittingly turned northward, where the welcoming sun rays filling the room through the partially open window were loudly suggesting that a dark night was always followed by a glorious day. Trying to break through the deadlock in his thoughts he went about the motions of getting ready to face the day that lay ahead like a zombie, totally insensitive to his surroundings.

* * *

Chapter 5

THE OUTBURST

The spark that was lit was now threatening to break into a consuming flame, engulfing both Charu's rationale and her emotions.

Though a wee bit unwillingly, yet the moderate in her was increasingly giving way to the extremist. The conviction that she had to write her own destiny was gradually growing stronger in her. She was now blinded by the vision that she was born to fulfill a significant and a very special mission in her life. She had come to the decision that she would do it, working along with the exiled armed wing in their camps that lay hidden in the deeps of those dense forests under the dynamic guidance of their leader, Arbindo Deka. It was becoming more and more difficult for her to identify with her earlier self as the fire in her continued to grow, threatening to assume grotesque proportions.

"Oh yes, peace! Peace is the final release. But then, there has to be war before peace returns. War is the inevitable price we have to pay to attain peace" – that is how Charu had begun to justify to herself, her charged emotions and her freshly chartered course of action.

Change! Change is inevitable. But then change for what? She was plagued by the present scenario. She was convinced that she needed to tread the unknown, the unfamiliar path in order to realise her dream. To capture her vision she needed to indulge this revolting streak in her. And this was the road for the time being that was leading her to the camps of the liberation forces across the borders of Assam. She was now determined to cross over to the marshy stretches lying at the foothills of the Durrung Ranges. But this was no simple cross over, for here lay the dual threat, the threat not only from the security forces but from the front liners of the liberation force who tightly combed this area. She was an unknown face for them. She was aware that once she would reach Arbindo Deka, then, the familiarity down the line would establish itself in no time. However, the passwords or the codes, much less the routes, were all unfamiliar grounds to her for the present. Charu was now in a hurry to reach the safe hideout of Mangal Doi, where she could take shelter in the house of Deka's nephew, Bijoy. From there, she would be under the direct jurisdiction of Deka to be briefed regarding the future course of her actions.

It was nearly 5.30 in the evening. The silvery twilight sent a cool thrill down her spine. Her first night away from her heaven, her house, the first eve of her self-imposed exile. Debojit's image, his outstretched arms, flashed through her mind but faded just as fast as the dense mist of the revolt in her spread across effectively obliterating his image.

She had reached outside a modest dwelling. The muddy, rain-washed, faded exterior comprised of crude, beaten bamboo blocks supported by even cruder, uneven bamboo posts seven to eight feet high. An equally rustic ladder made up of thick, flattened bamboo sticks lead to the front door. A thin beam of faint light ensuing from an oil lamp filtered through the several crevices that adorned the fragile structure that blocked the insides of the hutment.

"Bijoy", Charu called out from the bottom ladder. She waited a few seconds, getting no response she called out again. A small girl emerged from the rear of the house, her kohl-lined inquisitive eyes squinted as she suspiciously assessed the stranger. Then, she broke into a broad friendly smile, and, without uttering a word disappeared inside just as friskily as she had emerged.

The front door creaked open and a man in his thirties with stooping shoulders stepped out on to the ladder. He hurried down, crossing the steps with quick, sure strides and stood before her, hands folded in greeting. Her face lit up with a wide grin. It was Bijoy. "Welcome sister, we were anxious about your well being. It is a relief to see you here. We were beginning to grow worried, you know, the sun here sets very abruptly. It would have then become hazardous for you to move in these savage, unfriendly, marshy lands".

"Not to worry! I am here now", Charu responded, cheered as she followed him into the interiors of the house. Inside the dimly lit interior she was warmly greeted by both Bijoy's wife and children. "God, I have actually managed it here in one piece", she finally let out a sigh of relief all the while taking generous gulps of the coconut water offered to her and eagerly reaching out for repeated helpings.

After allowing herself a few moments of respite, Charu pulled herself up and got down to the issue at hand. She had no time to waste. Spreading out some crumbled sheet-plans which carried her ideas that she had systematically penned down on issues that were close to her heart, she addressed Bijoy, "you need to get in touch with your uncle at the earliest." Arbindo, Bijoy's uncle, was their guiding torch. Responding immediately, shouting across certain necessary instructions to his wife, Bijoy left the hut.

Sleep now finally threatened to overtake Charus' exhausted bones. Yet, so motivated was the soul that it refused to cave in to its call. Instead, requesting for a pail of water, she splashed water generously on her face and then went on to wash off the travel grime that covered her aching bones.

She finally noticed her shelter. She busied herself, carefully observing her frugal surroundings. What a come down it was from the luxuries of her well endowed home. This two roomed structure, as she could observe, had all the basic necessities. Crossing the rooms she moved into the cooking area where Sumita was busy putting together a simple meal. Charu's offer to help was politely turned down. "Ma'm you would be tired, why don't you catch a few winks, if you can? Out here the ground rules change, you know. We have to dispense with frills and social niceties. So, please, feel free, go and relax. You have a tough day ahead tomorrow", was Sumita's cheerful advice.

Bijoy soon returned to convey that the following day, they would start early at 3 'o' clock for her destination. So he advised that she needed to take an early meal and turn in for the day as it was imperative to cross the borders before day break. Those were the 'safe hours'. Even the most stringent outposts observed laxity in those hours with the police pickets on duty snatching a few hours of shut eye. Thus, these zero policing hours would hasten their movement through the wilderness to reach their camp.

However, a bevy of thoughts continued to race through her mind as the clock on the wall slowly ticked the hours by. She lay there in a restless state, switching sides every little while and reaching out now and then for a sip of the cool refreshing water from an earthen vessel placed conveniently by her bed side. Time seemed to have come to a stand still. It seemed ages before the clock chimed three, the hour resounding through the two small rooms of the hutment waking up the occupants of the rooms.

Groggy, Charu noticed a shadowy outline sailing through her room. The outline moved closer, slowly defining the features in the light of the small, lighted taper that the shadow was carrying in its hand. It was Bijoy. He whispered below his breath, "Didi, its time to get up and get moving." Charu gradually sat up. She stretched out her limbs in an effort to shed the lassitude that had finally taken over her spirit and then set about gearing up to face what lay ahead. Leaving the taper burning in a corner to facilitate her movements, Bijoy left the room quietly closing the door behind him. Moving to the corner, where a small plastic bucket stood half filled with water, Charu cupped her hands. As she splashed some water on her face to shake off the haze she managed to sprinkle some stray drops on her sari. Then wiping her face with the edge of her sari, she was done with the morning ablutions. As she moved back into the house, a mirror located in a corner wall caught her reflection. Instinctively, she moved closer and stopped to take a complete look. The bare vermilion parting which had gradually widened over the years due to the regular application of 'sindoor' stared accusingly back at her, yet failed to falter her steps. She moved past the room into the open, shedding her past without even the slightest evidence of remorse. Debojit was a forgotten chapter whose existence had ceased to matter.

"I think a cup of tea would help before we move", came Bijoy's mild intervention in her thoughts as he suddenly closed in behind her, holding a steaming cup of tea in his hand. Charu stretched out to take the cup and went on to lift it to her lips, oblivious to the scalding heat of its contents. Placing the empty cup on the lowest rung of the ladder, she started on the journey, purposefully matching Bijoy's steps with her own.

The moon streaked night guided their path. The cutting nip in the early morning air further quickened the pace of their fast strides. Charu keenly followed Bijoy close on his heels. Suddenly, a belligerent, threatening figure emerged from the lengthening shadows of the wooded opening, "Hey, state your purpose," Charu looked visibly shaken, taken aback by the sudden intervention but Bijoy seemed unconcerned and unruffled. Without slackening their pace he responded with a strange sounding term, possibly, a 'password'. The figure melted back in the shadows. As they moved on, it re-emerged with another, "This is Chetri, he shall guide you to Deka's camp". They continued. Charu was later informed by Bijoy that 'Chetri' had all the master ploys up his sleeve to successfully elude the police dragnets. He had perfected the art of finding his way through any police ambush being as comfortable with the entire terrain as he was with the back of his palm. He informed her that Chetri had also developed a close rapport with the nearby villagers that fell enroute and was therefore confident of a safe hideout, a shelter in case of an emergency.

Dawn was setting in, the moonlight intermingled with the first glow of the rising sun. Orange and grey streaks adorned the skies. As they finally crossed the borders, an expression of relief was clearly evident on Bijoy's features, as his pace unknowingly took on a more relaxed stride. The danger was considerably reduced with the spread of light. Visibility had gradually improved and now they could catch a glimpse of the top of a few hutments looming over the distant line of the horizon.

Excitement, intermixed with a growing sense of anxiety, resurfaced within her. Charu could feel her temples beginning to throb under the constant pressure of her burgeoning thoughts intertwined with conflicting emotions. A solitary image of Debojit once again ricocheted back into the mesh of the fast fading memories, as her confidence in the purpose that she had set out for, took complete control, sending through her frail framework repeated shudders of thrill in anxious anticipation. Her mind now finally stood conditioned and totally focussed.

The camp life was to be yet another eye opener for Charu. She had to cross at least four check points before she could gain proximity to Deka. She had not in her wildest dreams anticipated anything close to the stringent security network which Deka had laid down for the core group.

Charu was greeted by Deka. Then followed the introductions to the main core group members:

"This is Charu, a new entrant into our armed wing. She has so far worked with committed zeal as a leading member of our political wing and is fortunate to enjoy the blessings of our captain".

"Hail the L.F", Charu greeted. All the people around her stood up and greeted her back in a non-committal, mechanical, expressionless military salute.

However, the message had gone across. She was special, and to be trusted as a special envoy of the captain. Most of them had not had the good fortune to come face to face with the captain, who was the binding source of their motivation, the LF chief. Those that had had the opportunity to meet him in person had come away suitably impressed with their convictions further reinforced. They now lined up for individual introduction as Deka moved with Charu through their lines.

"This is Amritya, Code 'Lima - one', incharge of operations, the overall head.

And this is Vikranto, Code 'Tango - Double one', incharge of the recruitments and the training of our recruits.

Then Shuvral, Code Yankee - One double one', incharge of intelligence operations."

Charu's training had begun. The first lesson that she had learnt was that this was a carefully structured wing. She now understood that she needed to be familiarised with each wing in order to be formally initiated into the organisation. So far, Charu had had no clue where she was heading for. But the captain had already, very carefully, chalked out her role in their purpose. The instructions to Deka were crystal clear – she was tipped off as the Deputy Chief of their armed wing. Without her knowing it, she was being drawn into the core of the dangerous game, manipulated by the core players – the Captain and Deka. She would gradually now be propagated as the new chief of the armed wing. This was being done in order to make way for Deka's swift shift from this land of the bamboos to the greener lucrative pastures abroad. The captain had already sought for himself political asylum and was covertly manipulating the whole 'economy' of terrorism.

This hidden agenda apart, the gullible, enthused Charu was presented with a very different picture of the ground realities.

Charu's familiarisation commenced with a detailed briefing on the operation by Lima-one- "We have several groups equipped and trained for different operations. There are ten striking groups that are totally self sufficient and have been placed strategically at key areas", Lima-one briefed Charu, very meticulously indicating the places on the map placed on a wall, facing them.

"And what exactly is their strength and ability to strike?" Charu further queried with a curious and growing interest.

"Each of these groups has twenty carefully selected commandos. They have short range, medium range and selective long range weapons with improvised explosive devices. We have amongst us well trained snipers and sharp shooters too," Lima-one elaborated.

"Are they to be trusted?"

"Well, that is a difficult question to answer. Not all of them are to be trusted implicitly. However, the group commandos you can trust even with your eyes closed. These are those who have voluntarily joined our liberation front and their level of commitment to our cause borders on the insane. They will go to any extent to realise our freedom," continued Lima-one.

"But then, I fail to comprehend why have we inducted the less committed into our fold?" reacted a bewildered Charu.

"Our hands are tied as we are left with very little choice. We need people to die for the movement. The frontliners have to be recruited from amongst the youth. A few are placated with money as they are unemployed, while a few are desperate for a luxurious lifestyle. Unfortunately, there are only a handful who can be genuinely aroused to the cause", elaborated Lima-one.

"I think, you are right. We are stuck with a limited choice. I can see your point of view now. And then who judges a quick buck. Okay, besides this, what else do I need to know," Charu further probed.

"Then, we have also over the course of time developed local groups who can be mobilised in a moment of crisis. Otherwise, in normal times they continue to work in the villages. They are also vital in providing emergency shelters to our core group and they work as the underground information channels too", detailed Lima-one.

They had been moving across the camp as 'Lima-one' gave her a lowdown on their movements. Suddenly, Charu halted, noticing a familiar face amongst the strangers.

"Who is that?" enquired Charu, "I think I have seen him earlier with Tarun."

"Tarun, the MLA?"

"Exactly!"

"Well, then you are bang on ma'm. Now since you are a vital link in our armed wing, I have no reservation about sharing these things with you. The captain had secretly instructed us to provide extra cover to a few MLAs."

"How come?"

"We had even financed their election and ......"

"Even what?"

"Well not really......."

"Nothing really, what? What you've just confessed is that we have given our support to booth capturing.....?" Charu's eyes had widened in angry disbelief.

"You realise of course.......", giggled Lima-one as his face broke out in a shrewd fox like grin.

A deep faltering sigh escaped Charu, "Well, may be you are right in a way! We have had our hands tied down for the sake of the organisation. Yes! There have been occasions where we have funded candidates who could sometimes in the future further our cause in influencing the government decisions".

"So ma'm so! Let what has to be, be, and let us just move on to our briefing."

"Ya! I think so, you may please continue," nodded Charu.

"And now for our suicide squads........"

"Yea, please that is an important area. They must be fanatically committed souls, may be even insane to a point. May be we could even call them man made machines totally lacking in emotions, feeling....," Charu reacted.

"No, not necessarily! These are those who are genuinely motivated to our cause. We gradually manipulate their psyche. Being intensely emotional, they have a high susceptibility and with a continuous flow of the desired reinforcements, sometimes stimulated for days on end, we get the desired results. Yes, they are human machines who will do and die for the cause without the least remorse or hesitation. However, the chances of success in such cases are, unfortunately, only one out of a hundred. Recently, however, we had a different case......." elaborated Lima-one.

"Different.....meaning......?"

"The guy had contracted AIDS. So, the fellow facing the inevitable had willingly allowed himself to be manipulated into striking a generous deal with the captain. He settled for a sum of 2 lacs of rupees to be given to his family. He was willing to lead a suicide mission knowing he was to die very soon anyways."

"But then, how is it that our people are contracting AIDS?"

"No, they are not. We had encouraged a few HIV infected women to settle down along the border. This was a sly strategy to infect the members of the forces camping in those areas. These gullible fools in their desperation are often on the look out for these easily available local females," informed Lima-one.

"Oh! I see it now. And, this brainless toad fell prey to his own snare, that's funny! But then on second thought, isn't this truly base and immoral on our part?" resisted Charu.

"Okay, so what here would you state is the concept of morality? The state government reinforcing its plans with the central forces and cold bloodedly carrying out our death warrants. Would it be moral to spare them and look the other way while they kill us without the slightest remorse. How can you even consider sparing them, how can you even dare to spare a generous thought.......?" glared Lima-one.

"It is their professional duty to fight against us in our freedom struggle to gain an autonomous state. It is our fight against the institution and the political authorities, but to ...." reacted Charu.

"Well ma'm let us then leave it to be a part of the biological warfare", sniggered Lima-one with an evil grin. Charu, straight facedly, continued to maintain a non-committal expression.

Taking note of her obvious dissent, Lima-one divested from the volatile to the more placid issues and proceeded to now elaborate on their communication system, "Our communication is often intercepted by the police," informed Lima-one.

"But then, we are doing the same, aren't we? Infact, I want to congratulate you for the last month's operation in which our team successfully ambushed a Police Party".

"Ya, we were fortunate to have a solid informer and so we successfully laid the trap."

"Hey, but you better beware of that chap, your informer. I have very reliable information that he has been double crossing," informed Charu.

"Your information comes in a little late, my lady, 'cause he has already been bumped off."

"You mean you were already aware of it," exclaimed an incredulous Charu. She was taken aback by this piece of information. Yet reluctantly felt a newly found respect for the system which was, somehow, growing.

"Madam, this is a treacherous game. We have to keep our wits about us 365 days of the year. A moment's laxity can lead to our total annihilation. So, you better beware too. The Police is constantly laying out traps to capture our people. It is a constant struggle of wits. We have to keep shuffling our informers and so should you. You need to be on a constant move, you must make it a point to change the routes to be taken, even the hours of your movement should remain unpredictable. The passwords and the secret codes also need frequent alterations. Also, as an added precaution, let us pre-set the frequency at which we would be in touch," suggested Lima-one.

"Spoken like a true cop", Charu arrested herself midway realising she had reacted to the dialogue in the very way Debojit would have spoken. It was Debojit's modus-operandi. An embarrassed silence followed.

"Amritya........"

"Sorry ma'm, we don't use names, only 'codes' to address each other here."

"Aren't you impressed? I remember your name," in an attempt to lighten the atmosphere commented Charu.

"Hey ma'm, take this as a serious warning, no names here," remaining unimpressed Lima-one persisted. Suddenly, a sergeant approached them and saluted.

"Sir, I have vital information that I urgently need to pass on to you," addressing Lima-one.

"Go ahead,"

"Could we talk privately?" continued the intruder directing a sideways unsure glance at Charu.

"It's fine to say what you have to say right here. Speak out, sergeant," commanded Lima-one.

"Sir, Lima-II has been knocked off by a police picket this morning along with three more of our members at K-2. The Police have also seized our latest consignments of weapons and rations at K-4. It appears sir, we have a mole right amongst us," elaborated the sergeant looking tense and concerned.

"The bastards!" Lima-one's face turned a hot red. Seething with anger, he hissed, "I won't spare Ghoshal this time. The bloating creep is paid enough by us to turn a blind eye to our activities."

"Who is this Ghoshal?" Enquired a suddenly insecure, concerned Charu.

"He is the new SHO here. The rascal! How dare he play the cat and mouse game with us. We won't spare him now. You may leave, sergeant. There is work to be done ma'm, we will meet later," Lima-one moved briskly away, dismissively.

Charu returned to Deka's cabin where she found him already involved in an agitated discussion regarding their next moves with Tango and Yankee. The news had obviously reached him earlier.

"These isolated defeats do not worry me. They are not a serious threat, but then, why don't we manage to infiltrate the forces too? The Government, as you know, is recruiting most of the surrendered insurgents. Give clear instructions to G-17 to surrender along with his team and work at inveigling into the payroll of the government," strategised Deka.

"We must also immediately inform the captain to send in a fresh consignment of ammunitions and funds," came Yankee's concerned suggestion.

"We will arrange for the sending of the fresh consignment of arms, but money is an issue. We shall have to make the necessary arrangement to generate it on our own. Instruct Lima-one to activate the network and arrange for the kidnapping of a couple of those that have already been short listed," was Deka's seasoned instruction.

Charu intervened, "But that is not in our charter. We will land up antagonising the local folks...."

Deka directed a disapproving, piercing glance at Charu, effectively bringing her opposing, intervention to a grinding halt, "We shall tackle that issue later. I mean, we can take up the matter later and discuss it separately."

Returning to the issue at hand he continued, now pointedly ignoring Charus presence. "Go ahead, plan simultaneous attacks on the oil refineries, the Behari labour settlements and the concentrated muslim pockets. These are now our immediate targets. Heads need to roll. Clearly highlight all those sites that we had in our earlier discussions listed for an emergency drill. We shall be meeting again in half an hour," Deka had dissolved the meeting for the time being.

After their departure, Deka picked up the recently procured satellite phone to speak to the captain meticulously updating him with the latest development and their intended course of action.

"No absolutely not. You shall do nothing of the kind. We, have already activated our political lobby to push through the issue of banning the special operations group (SOG) of the Police in our area. Your suggestions may have very dangerous repercussions. No way, I absolutely prohibit this course of action. Drop it immediately and that's an order!", boomed the captain.

"But sir, there has been a lull far beyond their expectations. Cops are moving freely amongst us. They have taken to using the services of our own people by tempting them with monetary gains and assuring amnesty for their offences."

"No, I shall not allow it. Instead go immediately ahead and mislead the SOG into killing a few innocent villagers. Convince them with misleading evidence that they are insurgents. This will provide the required fuel to further strengthen our propaganda. Once the SOG is dismantled, the ball falls back into our court. The police and army camps are well targeted and plainly identified. And, anyways they always move in uniform, so they are sitting ducks for our people."

"You are the boss, sir, we comply," Deka agreed.

"Good! Best of luck then".

The phone line was disconnected. The satellite phones were truly a boon for them. Deka then immediately sent forth fresh instructions with the directions to wait for further orders. Yankee was called in to discuss another case of a delicate nature privately.

Charu was slowly getting acclimatized to what exactly was going on in the camp. With the advent of the dark, as the shadows lengthened, life within the camp took a round about turn. The freedom fighters now reverted to being ordinary, unimpressive men with all the possible ordinary, human failings. The weak human flesh was now taking over. Wine, women and wealth, the three essentials of failure and the sure shot antidotes to the success of their purpose were now conspicuously evident in the camp. Charu had long accepted that greed and carnal temptation would surely and effectively eat into the sturdiest of social structures. Charu could now feel the greedy caterpillar gradually gnawing away at the healthy leaves of their 'noble' movement.

Deeply perturbed, Charu retired to the privacy of her quarters. Sleep finally took over her troubled mind that was increasingly harassed by the glaring gradual displacement of goals that was creeping into their system.

The next morning the papers screamed out in bold letters the killings of five innocent villagers by the SOG and its terrible aftermath where the villagers had gone on a rampage lynching the SOG men and looting their arms and ammunition. The obvious outcome was the launching of fresh intensified mass scale combing operations by the police force.

Newspapers carried different versions. Some cried themselves hoarse, declaring foul play on the part of the SOG and demanded its immediate liquidation.

The Chief Minister, realising the sensitive nature of the present uprisings, gave his assurance to the errant leaders and announced its immediate withdrawal from the area.

Having been a part of the political wing earlier, it did not take Charu long to comprehend and clearly read the growing undercurrents.

The incidents which had taken place earlier, as masterminded by the military wing, flashed past. She infact, had already been prepared for some similar outfalls. But this! This went far beyond her comprehension. The poor naive soul had so far not been exposed to this dark side of the character of the captain and Deka. She had imagined them as the messiahs of the downtrodden. The pedestal on which her idealistic beliefs had placed them, took a beating and crumbled. She was also finding it very difficult to comprehend the SOG factor and how it could have been blown beyond proportions.

The newspaper reports and the dominant undertones clearly reflected the sustained effort of the Liberation Front spokespersons that were in constant and close liaison with the media elite. She was essentially in conformity with these manipulations, but, even the very thought of sacrificing the innocent, offering them up as bait, initiating the communal riots, kidnapping and torturing for ransoms perturbed her and distressed her to the very core. It went against the very grain of her sensibilities. She could not and would not condone such initiations. To strive for the realisation of one's dream was justified but the means adopted were unacceptable to her. Once she took over as the head of the military wing all this would stop, she kept reassuring herself again and again.

But the nagging fear kept gnawing at her insides, that the corrosive elements had already done irreparable damage, eating deep into the system, the web of deceit and greed had its tentacles firmly entrenched and she was realistic enough to accept that the web spun by the forerunners would not be easy to destroy. Now, there was no way out for her. Its vice like grip had her firmly in its hold. There was no retracting her steps and she knew her conscience would not allow her to keep pace with the present sham that had been set up. If she retracted, she realised that she would also become the enemy and a target in the hit list of both the cops and the Front. She would carry a hefty reward on her head and she would eventually lose her head at the hands of her own henchmen.

Once more, the bamboos were looming larger than life, threatening to snuff out their hopes of liberty. Freedom was fast becoming a distant dream, elusive and unreal. Her dream which had seemed to have begun to taking on a concrete shape, now, seemed reduced to mere hallucination. The bamboos continued to grow and were now beginning to pierce her insides. She felt drained. Had she made the mistake of projecting herself larger than life? Was she really meant to make that difference? Was she over stretching her potential? Was she meant to only keep rolling with the tide? It finally hit her. She had reached the crossroad where she was moving back and forth unable to decide or to move any further in her purpose. Her ideal stood fractured. She wavered........ Yet she decided to linger on.

The optimist in her gradually took over. After all, she justified, it was only her second day here. Probably, she had over simplified the goings on. May be there was another side of the picture that was still not unveiled to her. She still needed to identify with the rest, needed to get to know them all individually, work her way through each member whatever be their cadre, in order to get to the real picture. The curtains were still not completely withdrawn to reveal the real purpose. There were still miles to go before one could sleep and tomorrow was another day, another dawn. Her tired mind gradually drifted off to sleep......

★ ★ ★

Chapter 6

THE OTHER SIDE OF THE FENCE

Life after Charu had been a series of shocks for Debojit, but he was gradually making an effort to recover. Charu's leaving him suddenly in the lurch had had a shattering effect. He could still not fathom what had gone so wrong that she had felt the need to dump him like this. She had always been his world, his backbone, his voicing board, he had counted on her being around, whatever the circumstances and yet here he was left all alone to face the music. Could things get worse? Life seemed to have lost its meaning, yet he had to pull along. However hard and meaningless life may appear at a given moment, but eventually one always moves on. And that is what life is all about!

Life for Debojit was proving to be rather tough since Charu had joined the enemy, the armed wing of the liberation front. He had had a rough time proving his innocence that he had not been hand in glove with his wife and the militants. He had still not totally recovered from the aftermath of the shock that his wife had preferred to leave him destitute, deserting him in times when he needed her support the most.

But then life has a funny way of meeting situations half way. And so, something within Debojit now motivated him to become more focused on his job. His past goodwill had also helped to pull him out of the situation comparatively unscathed.

Insurgency affected different people in different ways, so also the police. The police could not, solely on its own steam, eradicate insurgency. This was a harsh fact that everybody including the police force was plainly aware of. The police actually acted as a repressive agency of the political governance through civil administration. It is also a well accepted fact that it is difficult, rather next to impossible, to find political solutions to such problems so soon. There are innumerable vested interests which are simultaneously at work. In the interregnum, the security forces, therefore, tend to contain disruptive forces which actually is a different ball game all together. There are hordes of players with diverse interests and each player tackles his turn in the game differently. So, Debojit too found himself oscillating between the means and the ends.

Debojit over the initial years had developed a reformative attitude. Hence, he believed in manipulating the given situation to lead to surrenders. But this was easier said than done. To get hard core offenders to surrender yet remained a distant dream. Such ideal situations never really happened. However, now and then one was successful in getting the front liners or the jobbers to surrender. Debojit always referred to this class of offenders as "jobbers" as he was aware that this lot was deployed by the militants for carrying out only specific chores and were never privy to their core operations. A few only performed the limited task of being "couriers" for a very limited purpose and time and were referred to as "helpers". This sect was inducted either via the lure of money and riches or they were compelled under some pressure tactics and threats to perform 'piecemeal' chores.

In so far as the 'financial' conduits were concerned, the police despite persistent and repeated endeavours had failed to discover provable links. Hence, it was almost not possible to prosecute this lot. As far as the counterfeit currency that was flown in was concerned, the routes and the passage were so efficiently covered that the police always failed to get hold of any concrete evidence and had to go by whatever hearsay information that managed to trickle in. The police woes, however, did not end here. The political wing of the insurgents though overt in functioning, could not be touched even by a barge pole as they had very strong though covert political linkages.

Hence, an attempt to sweep away the intricate webs deeply interwoven in the system was an extremely formidable and certainly a monumental task.

Circumstances, however, could often force a person to change drastically. They could wean him of so many values and convictions that he may have earlier stood for and Debojit was no exception. Now he had chosen his lieutenant, his right hand man, to carry out and enforce all the lowly and nefarious jobs necessary to evince the desired outcome to succeed in the given system. 'Jabar' was now his right hand man. Mr. Jabar had mastered all the tricks of the trade. He knew how to lure the insurgents through purchased informers, to play a double game to get the insurgents executed under some misappropriation or some slyly contrived sham. This was often also followed by getting rid of the informers as well, at a later more opportune date. In fact, they were sitting ducks for the police. So, they were shrewdly drawn into the police dragnet and at a suitable moment the police would satisfy their purpose, killing the birds with one stone. Thus, they would fulfill their mission subtly using one against the other. It was a case of two successful kills with one single shot.

If one had had the opportunity, to question Jabar on his mastery in this art of deceitful planning of these 'official' murders, Jabar would have confided, "Well, the victims themselves have taught me to play the game."

Jabar had himself been a victim of this game for long when the informers in sway would conveniently cross over for more lucrative gains. Jabar had also over the years mastered the 'use' and 'throw' techniques. And most surprisingly, through all this, Jabar had Debojit's blessings, who broadly masterminded the statistical depictions, once again then a circumstantial compulsion!

Only a few days back, an incident had taken place where the insurgents had in cold blood killed six innocent civilians and two security personnel. The highly volatile media immediately came in to foreplay. They generated unrestrained public criticism and political mudslinging, making all possible wild allegations and accusations.

The departmental pressures were also intensified. In an attempt to set right the barometer readings, Jabar employed his often tried and tested ploy. The police shot dead three criminals in a sly encounter recovering from them two Chinese pistols, two kgs of explosives and a detailed map of a petro-refinery. Thereafter, it was made a public declaration that the police had successfully pre-empted an attack on the refinery. And of course, the post encounter investigation trails were led to believe that those killed were the 'miscreants' who were behind the killings of the innocent civilians. The civilians were suspected by the liberation front to be working hand in glove with their anti group, the NBF, who followed ideologies that were radically divergent from those pursued by the LF. This was the reason propagated by the police to be the cause behind the innocent civilians' gruesome murder.

This 'balancing act' thus provided a breather to all, including the administration and of course the governing party. As has been the case, time and again, it is never difficult to draw the official support for such counter attacks as it generally encourages the generating of pro-official propaganda that point towards a committed administration. These moments are also suitably encashed to carry out effective and very strong anti-militant propaganda through the support of the media which blatantly highlights their nefarious tendencies and indulgences in wine, women and personal hoardings, both in the form of property holdings and other such sources of wealth.

Debojit was well aware that all these underhand tactics would bring only short term respite and could not provide any long term solution or permanent relief. Yet, he had long realised that one man alone could not bring about any major change in the system. His conscience still pricked him when he considered the slipshod and shabby manner in which the investigations were conducted and hence the core group of insurgents was never successfully ensnared into their dragnet. Rather, the short cut measures only created new victims of the official 'tricks' and resulted in more smouldering public resentment. But then, in all fairness, where was the time and the patience for effective in-depth investigations?

The reasons that had given birth to this typical police sub-culture were not really unfounded. Debojit himself had suffered its aftermath where he was faced with prosecution by his own seniors. There were two similar situations where his acts of commission in liquidating a terrorist were deplored for the reasons which resulted in four cops losing their lives. The memories were still fresh and vivid in his mind. Not very long back, he was the additional superintendent of the police. The Chief Minister's house had stood within his area of operation. He would periodically review and beef up the security of the state's topmost public executive.

Around 1700 hours on the 12th of August, barely three days before the Day of Independence, four insurgents infiltrated the outer cordon of the Chief Minister's residential security pretending to be some visitors from his own constituency. They were requested to undergo the regular screening procedure. But before they could be subjected to a physical check, one amongst them pulled out a silencer packed weapon and shot down the sentry on duty and the remaining three meanwhile rushed inside breaking the security barrier. They then took position at more strategic points evading immediate detection. The police personnel deputed on the spot were immediately galvanised into action. The man responsible for the sentry's killing was zeroed down upon and shot dead. Then ensued a heavy cross fire between the police force and the insurgents. Debojit was quick to reach the spot and take charge of the operations in a thorough and systematic manner. It began with his orders to curb senseless firing by the force lest it should result in innocent killings. He then went on to systematically cordon off the entire area in question, dividing it into clear cut blocks for the purpose of weeding out the insurgents and simplifying their identification. This was no easy task. The CM's house was crawling with a generous number of civilian staff, along with certain visitors who had now also sought shelter, scrambling for cover in order to evade falling victim to the spray of indiscriminate firing. It was no mean task identifying the actual intruders. The firing was brought to a halt and there now prevailed a threatening lull.

The fast setting sun in the glorified horizon spread illusionary shadows, making the picture more grim and elusive. The media, quick to smell the action spot, were already perched at strategic locations to cover the real life drama. The concerned senior cops along with the bureaucrats had assembled at a safe distance and were embroiled in a clueless brain storming discussion that seemed to be leading them nowhere.

Meanwhile, the slain intruder had been identified. This facilitated several crucial information inputs with regard to the organisation he had been the member of. It also increased the likelihood of the possible identification of his other gang mates. In the meantime, further supplements of the force had already arrived and taken strategic position. The intelligentsia did a good job analysing the possible identity of these hidden hands. Closely monitoring the progress, Debojit was successful in getting his commando team to surround the spot where the gang leader was hiding. A burst of gun shots that ensued from his end in self defence was immediately silenced by the commando sharp shooters. But, unfortunately, the explosives that he had in his possession were also detonated in the exchange of fire. This resulted in the blowing up of that spot and the surroundings that was now resembling a devastated battle ground.

As a consequence of the gang leader's demise, the remaining two miscreants came out of hiding with their weapons raised above their heads in a signal of surrender. But then considering the complex chain of events that had preceded this surrender bid, it would have been foolish to take any further risk. So, within split seconds, while the entire world watched the horrific scenario through the media, they were gunned down in cold blood. There spread a wave of jubiliation. The police force was applauded for its quick wit and able response to the crisis.

But this was not the end of the matter. The liberation front activists came into action immediately raising such a hue and cry over the human rights issues and declaring, "There was no possible justification for murdering them when they had offered to surrender," they screamed.

To add further fuel to the fire, the authorities dealing with the human rights ironically gave their consent, waving the green flag to the raked up issue and leading to an enquiry being conducted regarding the entire chain of events.

The deputed, over zealous enquiry officer, immediately indicted the cops on the scene. Debojit, for a while, retracted into a state of stupor. Then, in his defence, he cited the incident of Mangal Doi where in an encounter, only one militant had survived as all his gang mates had perished and he had then stepped out with an appeal for surrender. He was taken into custody after he had surrendered his weapons. He was then made to sit in the rear of a police jeep with four other cops. One of the cops carried a revolver in his holster. The surrendered person, yes, the militant Ricky that is what he was called, then cunningly proceeded to break ice with the cops. He presented a very moving picture where the adversity of his circumstances had forced him to join the militants despite the facts that he hailed from an influential family.

Unaware of his real game, the cops inadvertently eased and relaxed their vigilance upon him. Taking advantage of this, he stealthily drew out the revolver from the unsuspecting cop's holster and shot them all down in cold blood.

The resultant attitude of all and sundry then typically was, "Now where was the need to relent? He should have been shot as soon as he surrendered."

Under the police sub culture, the concept of special operating groups has also found favour as a covert operation. The militants who surrendered were very often lured into helping the police operations in lieu of the offer that the incriminating cases pending against them would be closed. Thus, they were,'then, included in the police team. They were taken in under the assumption that they would go back to moving in the mainstream, while for the time being they would be used to counter other insurgents. This was strategically useful as they were well versed with the modus operandi of the insurgents, and thus it facilitated the operations conducted against the exiled insurgents. The police action with the SOG delivered marvellous dividends, sending nervous flutters into the camps of the liberation force. They then mobilised the political wings to demand the dissolution of the SOGs by vehemently citing the few examples where the SOG forces had resorted to extortion or other similar transactions. The local administration was thus compelled to unwind the SOG system.

It soon became apparent that visual policing could never be as effective in such a scenario with the cops identifiable in their uniforms, official vehicles and movement. Thus, avoiding the police dragnet then became child's play.

Debojit had realised that as the police was meant to deal with crisis situations it could not adhere to too many standardised operating procedures (SOPs as they were commonly referred to). One had to take refuge in one's ready common wit to tackle the given situation. But, at the same time, not having SOPs also resulted in complexities vis-à-vis the non professional and the unscrupulous breed of cops. So, how did one control them? Moreover, SOPs also resulted in the birth of paper tigers in the force that would issue the instructions on paper, seek periodic reports and then conveniently punish for the non-compliance of the said orders. Thus, paper actions resulted in encouraging false data reporting and monitoring, more so in the armed units. It had become a mere façade where they would venture forth in the morning for patrolling and then conveniently return at meal time. It was a sad state of affairs as it was no longer a mile by mile scanning; rather it was reduced to a meal to meal monitoring. The counter insurgency operations thus fell victim to the numbers game. The effectiveness plummeted to ground zero. The reasons were far more complex than just the sub-cultural distortions that were being cited. The around the clock pressure, continuous long term deployment, removed for long stretches from ones families, a very taut and tight structured command system offering no possibilities of venting their pent up frustrations, so on and so forth, were also some of the major causes. The miserable living conditions further added to their woes, thus resulting in a gradual increase of the fear psychosis, particularly in the lower rung of the force. They were obviously not sufficiently sensitised to cope and override the multiplying pressures. Stress tends to lead to its own behavioral deflections at the lower levels – easy availability of a floating population along the borders, desperate to remain in the good books of the force, with their women becoming easy prey to the security men and the local political heavy weights. Of course, these carried with them potential dangers, for instance, a few of them would land up exchanging death warrants in the form of HIV/AIDS infections. A few even indicated that it could be a cleverly contrived game plan of the insurgents – this meant infecting the forces, thus announcing their death warrants. Alongside were other addictions as well.

Nevertheless, coming back to the brass tacks, Debojit was still working at holding the grenade by its lever. It was an accepted fact that even micro level impacts of modernisation were lacking in the forces, where as the insurgents were well endowed with far more sophisticated inventory and tactics. The forces were also handicapped by the fact that the formalised training given to the force did not provide them with an upper hand to capture the 'on the job' intricacies well.

The unfortunate odds, which Debojit and his team were saddled with, as an inheritance from their predecessors, did not make the job any easier. Once taking up these issues, he had cited these deficiencies before his seniors only to be interjected, "Are these problems cropping up despite your presence or because of you or did they exist earlier too?"

"No sir, these have now been there for a very long time," Debojit had replied.

"Then where is your problem?" sniggered the state chief.

Debojit returned to his chair brutally shaken. He felt bewildered with the complexity of the working concepts which now stood exposed.

He finally decided to retire for the day carrying in his mind a jumble of contradictions. When sleep came and took over his exhausted frame, was difficult to tell!

The unrelenting sharp ring of the door bell managed to pull him out of his bed. Just for a few minutes, Debojit remained unaware of his whereabouts. Then finally waking up to the frantic caller he looked at the clock – it was 2 A.M. Now what could it be? He hastened to the door and roared, "Who is that?"

"I sir, your guard", came the reply.

"Have you lost your darn head, what do you mean by ringing the bell like this?"

"Sir, I have been calling you for the last half an hour, but you were in deep sleep."

"Why? What's up?"

"Sir, there has been an attack on one of our company posts at Panihari. The camp has been attacked from all sides; the place is teeming with insurgents. The confrontation is still going on, but our people seem to be outrageously outnumbered.

His words worked like magic, shaking off Debojit's lethargy. He rushed indoors, changing into his uniform and placed his gun in his hip-holster.

Just as he was about to contact his subordinate in the police lines, his guard reappeared at his front door with further details, "Sir I have already alerted the quick reaction team (QRT). They are ready with the vehicles."

Debojit moved with swift purposeful foot steps down the long corridor leading to the front portico of his living quarters. His team was ready and waiting. They saluted him as he appeared. He immediately turned to the QRT incharge, Pronoy, an Inspector with a lot of experience behind him.

"Sir, we can't risk rushing in like this. It could be suicidal. One never knows......... they may have planted land mines enroute," warned Pronoy.

"Yeh! But, we also cannot abandon our people in the camp like this. We cannot leave them to face the music alone. We have to send forth additional supplement."

"Of course, we have to. That is right sir. We could instruct our Charlie and Delta companies to march to their aid from the north and the north west respectively," spreading the map before them Pronoy continued, "Sir, if we were to send them instructions to move their troops in, from these directions, they would possibly reach there faster", Pronoy pointed out on the map.

Carefully considering the strategy for a few seconds, Debojit nodded in agreement "Well, yes, but then they will have to move on motorcycles or may be on foot beyond Kaliteckri and beyond Tapol. There is a possibility of their being delayed. But, they have to take these measures to avoid the risk of being blown up."

"We could ask the Krishnai district incharge to cover the eastern side. They could wait in ambush, in case some of the insurgents should attempt to escape from there to the Karbi-anglong area where they have their other camps," Debojit voiced his concern.

"That is a sound strategy sir," beamed Pronoy nodding his head enthusiastically in support.

"They should also be instructed to carry along an ambulance with a first aid team. But, initially on approaching, they should be placed at a distance till the route is cleared for them", Debojit continued to bark out the directions.

"The doctor and his team will be ready by the time you mobilise the other troops, sir" Pronoy nodded in assent.

Debojit then got on to the wireless to give directions to his officers and to get in touch with the adjoining district officers, having to refer repeatedly to his diary to pick up the fixed codes for the different locations. After numerically determining his instructions, he frequently changed the channel speaking at random intervals. This drill had become essential as the insurgents had access both to their wireless net and the interceptors to tap the police movement.

Half an hour had elapsed and he had yet to make a move. A quick session of debriefing followed to ensure his men were well equipped and familiar with the essential codes and signals.

Debojit's directions kept tumbling out –

"Remove the vehicle... the convoy must maintain symmetry .... Where is my spare gypsy? I want it right here".

"Sir, I think its tank has not been refueled."

"Why?" reacted a flustered and visibly agitated Debojit.

"It was out patrolling till late last night."

"For what? And that is no excuse for an empty tank. I have briefed you on this issue earlier too," snapped Debojit impatiently.

"My mistake sir, but we can manage without the vehicle"

"Okay" relented Debojit, "And do we have the SLR (self loading rifle) as well as the mortars?"

"Yes sir and the QRT also carries an automatic grenade launcher."

"Great! But, how have we placed them, they are area weapons".

"Sir exactly as per plan – 2"

"Nice"

"And how do we move?"

"Sir, we are planning the convoy composition as has been arranged here. We shall keep moving all the time maintaining a safe distance – all our wireless equipments have been synchronised on the channel no. 3 – all likely communication has been adequately pre-coded and the operator in each vehicle has been properly briefed. Motor mechanics are there to immediately attend to any contingency, men are adequately protected with their security vests on, and each member carries 2-3 grenades in the front pocket of their dungarees for immediate use. All weapons have been thoroughly checked and loaded for action. Each member carries small quantities of dry rations and water bottles and, of course, as you would have observed, sir, they are all sufficiently camouflaged," bragged Pronoy.

"Well, okay I am convinced," intervened an impatient Debojit even before Pronoy had finished with the extravagant briefing.

"By the way, I have also instructed the Deputy Superintendent of Police (DSP) to place ambushes at strategic points on the possible retreat routes that may be taken by the insurgents. The DSP was of the opinion that this group probably belonged to the LF," Debojit thought aloud. "He is absolutely right sir; we really don't need to worry on that front. DSP Nagar Sahib is a sound strategist. He always does a thorough job, his implementation is always very thorough," nodded Pronoy assuring his harried Chief.

Debojit immediately proceeded with his convoy. They parked their vehicles a good 3 kms away from the camp on siege. The drivers took position standing guard, while the core party proceeded to move ahead.

Everybody had quickly taken position to move towards the Panihari camp. Time was ticking by. It was 4.30, very close to day break. The dark shadows enveloping the sky seemed to be slowly lifting. All this while, the intermittent bursts of fire from Panihari reverberated across the surroundings, as the team cautiously crouched closer.

The Panihari Camp commander, Hazarika, was in constant contact with Debojit. The latest update from him had informed Debojit of how after one of the insurgents had been gunned down, the firing had stopped from their end. The commander, however, was still unsure whether the insurgents had fled or were still in hiding. The temporary lull could also be a mere deception strategy. The camp, he had informed Debojit, was in complete shambles.

Hazarika warned Debojit repeatedly of the lurking dangers and advised their taking position at a safe distance. He still seemed surprisingly confident of being equal to the situation. He repeatedly announced to Debojit of his confidence in his team which, after an initial shock on being taken unawares, had quickly recovered and were now putting up a tough fight.

The morning glow was gradually spreading across the horizon forcing the dark shadows to give way.

With the approaching of dawn, Debojit moved on to the camp.

However, the scene there was heart wrenching. They stood there as mute spectators to the blood curdling sight that awaited them. The entire row of temporary hutments had been razed to the ground, blown off by the powerful blasts to smithereens, taking along with it two of the deputed police personnel.

It was confirmed that there were no less than seventy insurgents that had attacked the camp. Yet, the commander along with his men related with great pride how they had accomplished quite a feat warding off the attack. The loss of their fellow companions, however, dampened their enthusiasm somewhat.

Hazarika painstakingly narrated the entire proceeding, "After the evening's roll call had been completed, people dispersed in various directions. The night morchas were as usual activated and their respective positions taken.

Suddenly, around midnight, there was a surprise grenade attack on the camp. Two or three rockets successfully found their target, hitting our camp. For a while, absolute mayhem prevailed, fire bursts all-round, blurry eyed soldiers still in a state of undress, still unfocussed, not totally aware, scrambled out of their camp beds, no one had an inkling for a while of what had happened.

I had been penning down some notes at my desk when a rocket hit my roof leaving a huge gaping hole. Visibly shaken, I rushed out. Half the camp was on fire, the bamboos and the 'chatais' had fuelled an angry blaze, and the rest of the camp had already been blown away.

Waking up to the seriousness of the attack, I frantically barked out orders, positioning the by now alert jawans at strategic positions for counter attacks. Heavy cross fire ensued. The electrical connections had been blown away, but, the brilliance of the burning bamboos contributed to our becoming sitting ducks for the enemy.

Across the road visibility was poor, except for the momentary sparks that lit up its nearby surroundings when someone fired from the enemy camp. Gradually, it dawned on me that we were being attacked from all the three sides. I moved swiftly around the camp, in an attempt to bolster the confidence of my troops shouting aloud, "We'll get those bastards yet. Now that they have come begging at our door steps, let's give them what they deserve wholeheartedly. Ye ho! Keep on with your pot shots, my heroes!"

My cook in the meanwhile in his typical protective stance was following me closely and was wildly gesticulating in an imaginary attempt to ward off the enemy fire from hitting my person. I called out to him, instructing him to get someone to get me a mortar and a handful of grenades. Looking displeased, very reluctantly he moved to do the needful, hating leaving me alone for those few moments.

In the meantime, I had managed to calculate the approximate location of the enemy.

I gave my men clear instructions to fire from the fifty-two inch mortar which we have. It had an immediate impact. The insurgents withdrew to a safe distance. Meanwhile, my control room in charge had flashed across the message of the attack.

Sir, I'm afraid I must admit that the majority of my men were fast asleep after a hard day's labour. Their arsenal and weapons too were not placed in proper harness, as a result of which we lost some precious time while they geared up for an appropriate response. But sir, I must hand it to my men on the morchas. They have more than made up for this laxity."

Debojit patted Hazarika's back.

During the combing operations, the body of one of the insurgents was recovered.

And then, the word that was spread was – 'an attack on a police camp was unsuccessful. There was no loss of life. However, one insurgent was killed in the exchange of fire.' People accepted the version though very reluctantly. How was it possible for so many insurgents to combine their forces and cover so many kilometers and reach the camp unnoticed? It was gradually disclosed that they had collected in the nearby villages over an expanse of 3 days, taking shelter at various outlets and village houses as guests. Now that did not speak very well of the area dominance claims made by the forces. The intelligence had obviously been caught napping on their jobs. The police force stood exposed – lot of tall claims but very little content. It was evident now that it was all talk and little work inspite of the fact that they were tackling a highly sensitive area. The Police personnel had shown themselves in very poor light.

The dilemma continued to smoulder as this incident was swiftly followed by a series of five blasts that took place at vital points, one being within the police lines itself. This was a stinging slap on the face of the credibility of the force. Debojit stood perplexed. To embalm effectively and convincingly such a volatile wound was no mean task and he very well knew it. The repercussions were bound to follow. A do or die situation had emerged. The police Chief had gone ballistic. He was in no mood to lend his ear to any further explanations.

Debojit was fast realising that if the situation wa not brought under control immediately, heads would roll. The press was having a rollicking time, mocking the forces. Playing to the field, the extortion rates of the insurgents had also sky rocketed now, glaringly exposing the loss of faith of the common man in the security system. The rich were now willingly contributing to the insurgent coffers to ensure their personal security. They had made their choice – they anyways would have to pay tax to the government, so, much rather extend protection money to the goons. These developments were gradually shaking the very roots of healthy governance. Debojit's dilemma pursued, there were no signs of a let up.

Sensing an acute onset of demoralisation in Debojit, one of his juniors, his second in command, a very committed and aspiring officer who had gradually with due reasons developed a strong feeling of regard for his superior, came up with an effective game plan.

He had approached an informer who was willing to hand over four insurgents alive to them in exchange for a hefty sum of five lacs of rupees, as the insurgents in question were truly dreaded and very high on their hit list. Quality products always fetch quality price. The deal was sealed. Now the question arose, where were they to source the money from? Government funds have no provision for such a purpose.

Debojit considered the issue for a while and then he made two phone calls each to illustrious tea estate owners. Soon the issue was settled. Within a lapse of three days the agent had reported back to Debojit informing them of their modus operandi. The operation was now launched. It began with the picking up of all the four in question from a joint that had been formerly agreed upon by the informer. He had successfully crossed over. The police was immediately galvanised into action and the bodies of all the four were now recovered along with cleverly implanted explosives, weapons and a detailed map of a refinery on their person. It made headlines in the next day's newspapers. Their purpose was served and their credibility reestablished. The police was again back to working on solid ground. However, next in their agenda was the successful enactment of a game plan to knock off the informer as well, thus, removing once and for all any chances of exposure. He was skillfully, without his realising it, handed over as bait to another security force active in that area. They too benefited, with their score of killings graph showing an upward trend. After all, it was mere statistics which announced the success factor at any given time.

* * *

Chapter 7

RETALIATION

Assam has been a witness to successive phases of migration most of which have taken place to appease the multifarious wants of the predominant stake holders. Most obviously, it has been governed by the principle of the demand and supply factor.

Initially, the growing need for cheap labour in the imposing tea estates that covered a wide expanse of land and spreading as far as the naked eye could see, had probably been responsible for pulling in workers from the vicissitudes of the neighbouring states. But very soon, the immigration profile had undergone a major change and was now catering to the cheap gimmicks of the diverse political vote banks.

Side by side, multiple human settlements had gradually mushroomed disturbing the demographic balance and also creating a comfortable base for foreign spies to successfully unfold their operations in the given areas here and smoothly realise their designs.

Then, one could also clearly perceive the Jehadi influence finding its firm roots, continuously flowing in from across the connecting borders of the neighbouring countries. With the advent of these foreign players, the vicious game of terror had now taken on a far more bloodied hue.

However, in the meanwhile the LF had been repeatedly making organised attacks on these new upcoming settlements in an effort to achieve its multi-pronged plethora of objectives.

So, on one hand it was sending across the message loud and clear to the common masses that the LF meant serious business and was sincerely assisting their cause to dislodge the outsiders, who were encroaching upon their local resources and taking control over the life of the locals and the aboriginals. On the other hand, it was also grinding its personal axe by sending jitters through the government circles through these repeated acts of omission and commission. At the sametime they were encashing on the situation and acquiring more and more funds and weapons from the foreign sponsors by abetting their spread of terror and disquiet across the region.

Debojit's piggyback ride on the horses of success was unfortunately brought to a grinding halt. He had barely been able to enjoy the pat on the back that he had achieved through a carefully staged encounter, in which, those that had been exterminated were actually active working members of the LF. This had obviously incensed Deka. Simmering with rage and frustration at his unsuccessful attempts to nab the informer who had switched his loyalties and crossed sides, Deka now meticulously conceived and successfully implemented a new strategy. This gave rise to a serious local issue for the administration. Deka's men, in the wee hours of morning, around 4 am when there is generally zero policing everywhere, carefully conducted a well laid out operation targeting a labour colony in Gwalpara which was a Bihari settlement.

Suddenly, two consecutive explosions riveted the air followed by concurrent gun shots. Nobody had the slightest clue of what had transpired for quite sometime. The brilliance of the explosions had lighted up the skies for a few moments followed by a trail of agonising screams and wails of the victims it had left behind.

The occupants of the sparsely staffed nearby police chowki had, after careful consideration, decided to stay away form the scene. Being only two in number, the cops refrained from venturing out to help under the fear of being outnumbered. However, from a safe distance they observed a group of about ten armed men retreating from near the place where the blast had occurred a few seconds after the unfortunate explosions that had hit the unsuspecting Bihari community settled there. The cops, however, had informed the SHO in charge whose living quarter was located about five miles away from the chowki.

It was close to 6 a.m. by the time the details of this mishap reached Debojit. His telephone attendant on duty woke him up and narrated the details of the happening. Caught unawares, it took Debojit a few seconds to get his bearing right and to let the gravity of the situation sink in. This meant very serious repercussions. He was hit hard by the realisation that the consequences could be very far reaching. His sixth sense warned him that this would mean the loss of at least a dozen lives and at least 30-40 people grievously injured or incapacitated, not considering the collateral damage to the hutments in the locality. He demanded further insight into the situation but any more details were unavailable during the time he got ready and left for the location.

All this while Bordoloi, his SHO of the chowki carefully avoided coming face to face with his boss. He purposely avoided him, pretending to be pre-occupied with the demands on hand, the required relief measures to be implemented and the process of accumulating incriminating investigation leads. He realised that he had seriously slipped in carrying out his official duties. He should have been camping at the police chowki rather than enjoying a night out with his family. This was a serious lapse in the course of his official code of conduct and he was well aware that unless cleverly maneuvered it would have serious reprisals. There was no denying that if only he had been present at the police station it was possible that they could have saved a few of the unsuspecting victims from the aftermath of the debacle. So, he was gradually preparing himself for any eventuality. He fully realised that if Debojit should become privy to his serious lapse of responsibility, he would not be saved from his wrath.

Even before Debojit's motorcade had reached the spot, out of the blue materialized an entire platoon of soldiers busying them in an attempt to clean up their self realized mess.

Yet the scene that unfolded itself before Debojit's eyes on his arrival would shake any decent human being to his very core, blood curdling screams rent the skies, distraught mourning widows unaware of those present around lamenting the magnitude of their personal loss, orphaned infants hanging on desperately to their mothers' resisting bosoms, amputated, disfigured human remains crying out desperately for help and relief. Debojit's eyes gradually absorbed the scene. It was arrested by a sight that made him flinch. He wanted to flee the spot. Whatever had remained of a boy possibly around 12-13 years of age was hanging in mid air, trapped between two sharp iron wedges that had pierced through the little that remained of what had once been his neck. The surrounding flesh and bone had been yanked away with the impact, his bloody eyeballs seemed to be popping out of their lifeless sockets, his left leg had been brutally amputated and the copious blood that oozed had formed a huge puddle just below where the child hung suspended in mid air.

As far as the eye could see, blood, dismembered remains of human limbs, gory residue of entwined human intestines sprawled all around, shredded and tattered blood soaked remains of clothing that had once adorned the slight frames of the Bihari labourers. Some could be seen digging in this human mess for their brethrens; some were desperately looking for their kith and kin- for their untraceable parents, sons, daughters, spouses. Every ashen face seemed to be moving through this horrendous human disaster in a daze lost to the world and those surrounding them.

Whatever remained of the spartan dwellings that had once been shelters of the Bihari clan was another eye sore. The Kachcha dwellings now lay in shambles, the impact had not only blown its human occupants to smithereens but also probably their pots and pans had rocketed through their thatched roofs leaving behind huge gaping holes in them.

Debojit could take it no more. His insides had begun to revolt. A churning sensation began to grow within him, unable to keep the feeling down any further he returned and threw-up wretching violently. Repeated exposure to similar horrifying sights with human guts sprayed all over still bothered Debojit. He had still not become immune to such inhumanity. Humans were strange creatures. Debojit felt drained, sapped of energy but there still remained a job to be done at hand.

Bordoloi stood up in deference and saluted his approaching boss, Debojit. Before Debojit could express his displeasure Bordoloi started rambling his report–

"Sir, a total of sixteen people have been killed in the blasts and forty two seriously injured. The bodies have already been sent off for postmortem procedures while the injured have been shifted to different hospitals in the vicinity.

"Come straight to the investigations," cut in Debojit obviously in no mood to be humoured.

"Yes sir, of course. If you will please follow me, I would like to show you a few of those spots," so saying Bordoloi moved inside the colony followed by Debojit.

A very basic, primitive set up of 'Bashas' could still be seen standing, though on drawing closer it became clearly apparent that the bamboo structures had long out lived their lives.

The roofs of two of these structures had been blown off with the impact of the explosions. Bits and pieces of the items that had been a part of the 'Bashas' had been ripped apart as a result of the locally made rockets that had exploded within them.

"Sir, this particular crater is a result of the impact of one of those rockets that fell here. The remnants of the other can be seen wedged in the projecting stem of one of the coconut trees in the cluster there." Bordoloi was earnestly pointing with his right index finger towards the coconut tree on the right placed a good ten fifteen feet away from the 'Bashas'.

"So ...., this clearly indicates that these people have also used rocket launchers. Could you determine the number of the rockets fired in the attack? What about the direction and the position of the launchers? We need these vital details to enable us to come to a sound deduction. Half baked information shall get us nowhere," Debojit directed an impassive look before moving on.

Bordoloi taking quick strides in an attempt to keep up with the pace of his boss continued further, "Sir, we have already worked in that direction. After very careful consideration and taking a clue from the direction of the rocket remnants found embedded in the stem of that tree we retraced our steps backward from the spot and after covering about 3000 metres or so we noticed multiple footprints, Also the spot was strewn with carelessly thrown paper and plastic wrappers. Interestingly, we have also found the empty covers of a few cartridges of the .32 bore," not waiting for Bordoloi to complete his low down Debojit had moved towards the probable direction of fire. Bordoloi quickly followed suit continuing with his explanation. It was obvious for all to see that he had been caught on the wrong foot and was now trying really hard to cover lost ground.

Debojit was very minutely conducting a detailed survey of the situation. Gradually, as a clearer course of action was emerging after a point via point revaluation of the attack, it was becoming more and more apparent to Debojit that their modus operandi in this operation had been exactly a replay as observed in the earlier two similar attacks on Bongaigaon and Nalbari very recently. Just when Debojit was carefully pondering over how he needed to address the situation, what would be the best course of action to take, what should be their reaction, what control measures needed to be carried out, what were the safety issues to be tackled, his communication centre then forwarded the information, that as per one of their successful capture of their intercepts of the LF, it had become clear that the incident had been conceived and conducted by the LF activists working under the code name of 'Papa-22'. It was also discovered that seven of the main activists had now managed to escape to the hilly terrain leading to the land of Shillong.

Reinforced with this vital piece of information, Debojit immediately galvanised into action. He immediately forwarded orders to those concerned to bring together their chosen groups for these operations. His immediate reaction was to rush back to those areas and launch a massive hunt for the escaped miscreants.

In the meanwhile, unnoticed by him, a huge group of the kith and kin of the deceased and the local leaders had gathered surrounding him and his men. They cordoned off his passage and started shouting obscene slogans. Debojit stood baffled for a few seconds, then gradually started reorganising his thoughts to the immediate crisis on hand, a crisis that had caught him completely off guard. He had been so obsessed with his plans in Shillong and thereabout that he had totally let slip the possibilities of an adverse chain reaction against them from the local leaders and the aggrieved relatives of the victims.

Straining his ears he could now decipher the sharply worded slogans, "Down with the police force', 'they are mere posers', 'they care not for our safety','they are a spineless, ineffective lot', 'shame on them'.

The Gwalpara Business Association too, in the meanwhile, had grandiosely announced a 36-hours bandh.

Debojit was aware of the laxity on the part of the existing police force in the attached chowki. He realised that the act of omission on the part of the Chowki Incharge was unforgivable. How could anyone justify such a well contrived mass scale attack on a large community living a stones throw away from the police station.

But then, this would not be the right time to take up cudgels against one's own clan. He dared not rake up this issue now. It was an internal matter that needed addressing, yes, but not just yet. This would have to wait for later. There were more pressing issues to be dealt with immediately.

Debojit noticed the local sub-divisional magistrate standing there and watching the goings on from a safe distance. Debojit raised his hand in a gesture of salute acknowledging his presence. Greeting him loudly, Debojit moved within his ear shot with a volley of questions. "Where is the DM Saheb at present?" "Why don't you go ahead and announce a decent compensation package?"

"I think we should sir. The DM Saheb is on his way here. In fact, he has already contacted the government and got the green signal to declare a compensation package of a lakh each for the dead, and a sum of Rs. 10,000/- to the ones injured in the incident. He will be here any minute to make the formal announcement. In fact, we have been given ready cash, so the compensation will be handed over right here to the aggrieved on the spot", the SDM made the grand declaration. Satisfied and realising that they had made some headway in their attempt to save their faces, Debojit now directed his attention to the angry crowd, "Look, I am shocked at what has happened. I must confess even at the risk of facing your ire that we are equally aggrieved by your personal loss. We shall leave no leaf unturned to nab the assailants. We take a solemn oath here amidst you that we shall not let these insurgents go unpunished. No one shall be allowed to get away scot free. We feel and share your pain. But if you should hold us back here, we are losing invaluable time which may actually be allowing the insurgents to move beyond our reach. Time is of the essence. Please, do pay heed to our earnest urgings. Let us pass, so that we may immediately launch a major offensive against the miscreants. None shall escape. Please help us to help you. I beseech you permit us to leave," Debojit's voice was breaking up, trembling with emotion.

"We will not be satisfied by mere words. We don't want your verbal assurances alone. You stand there, and speak eloquent of being allowed to do your duty. Where was this awareness when your men were missing from their duty posts? Now you stand here and grandly announce your sincerity," screamed an old voice from the crowd.

"Yes, I shall not deny that, our men stand guilty on that count. And let me assure you, that this serious lapse on their part shall not go unaccounted for. They shall have to bear their cross for this failing. Please leave that to me now. I assure you justice shall be done. Trust me and let us help you," beseeched a desperate Debojit.

Bordoloi had clearly distanced himself from the scene realising that if the crowd should perceive his presence amongst them, there would be hell for him to pay.

Debojit's repeated pleadings finally made a breach in the threatening stance of the gathered crowd. Softening considerably, they finally allowed Debojit and his troops to pass. Debojit quickly proceeded to move to the police station where Bordoloi had already reached and sensibly putting his years of experience to use, had already gathered the required data and papers necessary for his boss to further his plan, to trace the insurgents now on the run.

Debojit carefully browsed through the map, outlining the possibilities of the escape route and the details of the terrain. Then he proceeded to contact the SP, Shillong, who expressed his willingness to support and extend all possible help in the operation launch. Thus, a carefully monitored joint operation was now underway.

However, nothing in life is simply black and white. There are always distinct shades of grey that hamper the smooth routes of success. Here, the jungle routes that they would have to cover were in major patches of LF dominated territory. This made the police patrol progress very difficult as here they were easy baits. The LF could very easily make mince meat of the police troops as they laboured through their territories. They could lay out landmines to blow them up, lay an ambush on the unsuspecting security forces, put misleading evidence thus leading them on a wild goose chase or even more seriously lead them right into the heart of their killing zones.

Realising the grave risks involved, Debojit decided to take on the responsibility on his own shoulders to personally brief his operation squads to follow certain precautionary dictates. They were given clear cut instructions to avoid the routine tracks, they were given due orders to take the off beat tracks.

Though involving much more effort and tedious wastage of time they were not allowed to ride on motorcades but track the insurgents on foot, keeping a safe distance between them.

Then they were given strict orders to avoid the natural shelters like the pariah. They were to keep constant contact with each other and with the headquarters, i.e. Debojit, so regular communication was declared essential. But unfortunately despite the fact that Debojit and his men made serious inroads their effort bore no fruit at all. Finally, the operation was called off, ending on a very sour and frustrating note – each police party merely ended up finding fault with the other. The end was – no result.

Sadly, inter force and inter-border coordination has always posed a serious problem. Either it is because of 'it is not my job psychology' when taking up 'areas of responsibility of the others', or it could be the 'one upmanship tendencies' that overwrite all the lessons taken on teamwork, national interest or selfless sense of public service.

Then, the mushrooming training camps of the insurgents across the international borders really complicated the issues further. This was one area where the police or the security forces could do very little to stem it. The only slim possibility that could help in this issue was through diplomatic initiatives to compel the government across to flush them out and hand them over.

Anyways, these remained the larger issues that needed to be addressed at a more opportune moment.

For the present, Debojit's job was to first and foremost ensure a more sound, more active, a more alert, dutiful and positive response at the 'chowki' level. This needed careful re-evaluation and garnering together of the forces he held under his sway.

Debojit was impatiently waiting for his forces to return in the evening.

The next operation to be launched was planned for 3 A.M. in the wee hours of that morning.

In the intermediate hours Debojit had wisely decided to personally brief his force. This waiting time bore precious dividends, as Debojit with nothing really mapped on his agenda during the period, spent the hours hobnobbing with the locales who on sensing the genuineness in his act, gradually opened up, warmly responding to the positive overtures they were receiving from him. Debojit had learnt his lessons well – if you truly wanted to win over the hearts of the local people, become a part of them and they will soon take over as your own eyes and ears. There was no denying the efficacy of this management policy, very soon he had them literally eating out of his hands. Thus, he had successfully implemented the golden managerial rule that community oriented policing even in the worst insurgency prone areas would prove to be an effective force multiplier.

Then, Debojit further decided to share his meal with the cutting edge level constabulary. When officially organised, it is addressed as the 'Bara Khana' in which the senior and the junior alike share their meals coming to a common level in the force.

But today, this was to be an informal, impromptu get-together. Without any prior announcement, with not even his immediate subordinates having any clue to his intentions Debojit discreetly strolled into the common mess of the constabulary during the dining hours and quietly took a seat. For a few seconds, his presence went unnoticed. Then the whisper spread across, 'the big boss is here amongst us'. People reacted, flustered and confused, they stood up at attention. Debojit laughed, "Am I such an ogre that I take you away from your meals. I am ravishingly hungry. Can you spare me some? I am not a big eater".

Peals of laughter resounding across the entire length and breadth of the mess broke the uncomfortable worried silence. It had been a masterly stroke and it was to have far reaching consequences. He had made a direct entry into their hearts. With this sweet thoughtful gesture he had won half the war. The meal started and ended on a merry note, light hearted banter, silly jokes shared over dal, road side songs and even personal issues were the talk of the meal.

Debojit, the leader, had made successful inroads into their hearts. He was well aware that their hearts would now over sway their minds. This team was now going to 'listen' to what he had to say to them, not merely 'hear' when he addressed them.

He crossed his fingers hoping the human touch would make them persuade the public to respond favourably to his leadership too.

Debojit along with Bordoloi and his team then conducted a short post prandial meeting. He returned from the meet with a smug expression on his countenance. The tide finally seemed to be turning in his favour.

The morning events had left him rattled and unsure of how his fate hung in the balance. After the fiasco, his seniors and even the Chief Minister of the state had given him a serious dressing down. They held him responsible for the terrible act of carnage that the LF had committed last night. He had stood before them like a puppy whipped hard for his erratic code of conduct. The prospects had then appeared bleak and threatening.

But now he felt re-energized. Next day would bring with it a greater charter.

* * *

Chapter 8

THE DOGMAS

Life, like water, moulds itself into the shape of the urn that holds it. Debojit was no exception to this essential side of life. During the course of his life, he had gradually travelled a tardy distance traversing from his personal abode to the professional abode. Gone was the emotional irate that made him susceptible. He had gradually undergone a total personality metamorphosis along with a radical change in his inherent convictions. Now, with a sharply attuned eagle's perception, he could detect the possible outlaws and then move on to mastermind the kill.

Today, like most days, his hands were full with the pressing work on hand. He had to put together and brief his team regarding an important mission. He was in a tearing hurry to reach his operational briefing room at the Headquarters. His car came to a grinding halt at the portico where his second-in-command was already awaiting his arrival.

"Good morning sir", he greeted.

"Morning......, are we ready for the meeting?"

"Of course, sir,"

"Then, what is the delay, let's move," came the impatient interjection.

Debojit's swift stride carried him into the conference hall. The room was aesthetically adorned all along with carefully cut bamboo panelling which had begun to lose its sheen. All those awaiting his arrival in the hall rose to greet their boss.

"Good morning, please take a seat," Debojit cast a cursory look across those present before settling down in his own chair. All others followed suit resuming their respective seats. After the usual quick shuffle of chairs there followed a pin drop silence. "Well, let's see, we will begin with the Deputy Commandant, Intelligence's latest inputs," Debojit shot a sharp look at Tapan, the officer in question. A universal sigh filled the air, interspersed with a few suppressed giggles. Most of the time, these inputs were just 'dra.. dra.. dra..' lengthy, monotonous, irrelevant with hardly any meaty facts imparted. Most of it was based on mere possibilities, with little or no light thrown on practical and possible action plans, which were what the field officers were desperately in need of. Yet, they could not afford to discount even the most inconsequential inputs. They were well aware, each one of them, that these irrelevant and seemingly unimportant issues could surprisingly help in drawing out a wider spectrum within which the executing force may draw out its road map. But, today was an exception. Tapan was well informed and suitably prepared for the occasion. He had with him substantive information.

"Good morning. Intelligence inputs are indicating a shift in the power base of the insurgents. The military wing of the LF under the leadership of Deka is trying desperately to severe connections with its political wing. If that should happen, it will be to our distinct advantage, and we can then exploit the rift between them. However, a few MLAs of the ruling alliance, who had won indirect support of the LF, are mediating. We are keenly tracking their movements and, as of now, on a need to know basis, we will be passing on the required inputs to the concerned officers for suitable repudiation. We have detailed information of the Women Cadre also joining the military wing of the LF."

Tapan suddenly faltered, noticeably breaking the swift momentum of his inputs as he realised that he had just mentioned Charu, the wife of his own General who had deserted him and joined the revolutionaries. She had now become one of their major threats, a force to reckon with. But Debojit appeared unaffected. He had made it amply clear to his department that 'she' was now their 'common foe' to be treated as such too. Looking back at his fault free, immaculate past integrity and record, no one dared raise a finger at his bonafides.

Taking control of his uncertainty, Tapan continued without a tremor – "We need to reorganise and prepare our forces accordingly. We should seriously now consider training our Lady Cops for counter insurgency operations. As has been recorded at the other locations, the possibilities of allegations of sexual harassment against the men in the forces cannot be denied or ignored.

The LF is also taking up focussed drives through their political wing to cleverly garner the support of the common man by particularly focusing on the backwardness, where there is a complete paucity of essential facilities, a total lack of development in those areas and discrimination against their lot. Through raking up some cases of police encounters with the support of the human right activists a growing sense of hatred, anarchy and alienation is being encouraged against our forces.

Then, gradually over the years many pockets and areas are now inhabited by infiltrators – the Muslims, Bengalis, Biharis and the like who were also brought and settled here by penny pinching, benefit conscious 'business communities' to provide cheap influx of labour and also by some conniving, shrewd politicians to boost their vote banks. The latest feedback reveals that a plan is also underway to hit these unsuspecting settlements and thus further inflame and spread communal disharmony and violence. This could be for two distinct reasons – firstly, to distract the attention of the administration here and, secondly, drive them away from the area. That is about it. Thank you very much sir", finishing his debriefing, Tapan sank back into his seat.

Debojit, a responsible Commander, scanned his entire team of workers, carefully observing and patiently waiting for their response. "Sir, we cannot afford to lose the general public support. It is essential for our success. If we allow the LF to successfully move the common man in their favour, it would deem serious trouble for us. We need to now work at effectively chiselling away at their increasing support. A laxity on our part at this crucial juncture would undoubtedly prove to be the nemesis of our government. All our support systems would begin to weaken, cave in and crumble, our informers would switch sides. Then our opponents would have convenient access to foolproof hideouts, and the support of the local dwellers to even attack the security forces," eulogized one of Debojit's old hands.

"You are so right. This problem is for real and is, as of now, staring us right in the face. We need to revamp our strategies and suitably react," supported Debojit.

Then the suggestions began to pour in. "We should undertake a strategy of counter propaganda. We need to now exploit their weaknesses. We have adequate data with us. The photographs of them womanising, wining and boozing would speak volumes on our behalf. Records of those amongst them who have indulged in nefarious activities abroad, sought dubious pleasures could reinforce our own case against them", suggested one amongst them.

"Another possibility is that a suggestion be made to the government to assign clear cut developmental roles to the forces deployed here. As it is, the civilians fearing militant reaction have avoided working in the remote areas. Since our units are anyway deployed there we could very easily undertake developmental efforts for the upliftment of the locals. Thus, having provided solid proof of our positive intent and effort for the uplift of the local communities. They then would automatically repose faith in us and our intentions. As of the moment, they abhor our presence here and, therefore, any amount of propaganda drives against the militants would not win us their ears and sympathy and would only beget an adverse reaction or a plain 'royal ignore' by these communities", asserted another.

"But why assume that the bureaucracy will relent and agree to pass on these powers to the police personnel?" questioned someone.

"So what then? We have our own funds allotted for community welfare action programme as well."

"Oh, come on, get real man! Are you really so ignorant! Those funds are mere pittance, with such resources in our hands we will only be able to provide some patch work, which is not going to win us their sympathy and approval. Hardly anything substantive. No it will not be enough to even scratch the surface," protested another.

"And then, why do you forget who would allow the money to be released like that? No way! This is all the economics of terrorism! It has now evolved as a lucrative industry. Everyone is eventually the 'Gainer'. This is only a small faction of a major game plan. So do you truly believe that anyone is even a wee bit interested in the betterment and the plight of the common man?" retorted a senior official.

Debojit was fast realising that the discussion was getting them nowhere. They were only losing invaluable time. The pendulum of the clock was ticking the hours away without any clear resolve surfacing!

But then, the crux of the issue still remained that what was being said was the harsh, unfortunate truth. Different lobbies had different stakes in this whole game plan. But then, whatever, Debojit's duty required him to contain the insurgency effectively and that he was determined to do. He would not relax his plans. Just then, he overheard another saying – "Here, we are planning our moves risking our very lives, while all this while the present regime is said to be considering going in for a peace accord with the bloody insurgents. If that should happen, they would then become our superiors under that settlement accord. Can we allow these bloody, blubbering, spineless lot to make us dance to their tunes? Well, I'll say........... never!!"

"Enough" thundered Debojit, "snap back to our agenda!"

What followed was drop dead silence. Debojit's sharp, high pitched tone pierced the silence – "So what is new in what you are saying? A state of warfare cannot last forever. Peace settlements are an eventuality. This is how societies grow and develop. This is how democratic institutions originate and find a firm hold. If they are not pressurised, then do you see the LF coming to the peace table, they would much rather subvert the whole system. Such academic talks are fine over a coffee table to kill spare hours but we here have serious business to attend to."

Realising that the Chief meant business and was in no mood for any fruitless banter, the entire group switched over to an alert and receptive mode. A few, though now unhappy, felt that they were left with little choice.

Debojit, taking charge, began to draw out a road map.

"Coming down to brass tacks, we shall, first and foremost, further create 5 special operation groups at locations M, K2, F5, T and S6. We shall also include in these teams a special component of lady officers. To deal with the threat of IEDs and mines, we need to drill it hard into the heads of our men to strictly follow the norms set by us. They are to either walk covering the flanks or are to use motor cycles.

An advance party is to always move ahead, sanitising the areas to be covered so that the entire group is not exposed to their lethal threat. Once the road opening party has given clearance, then only our men would be allowed to venture forth. Popularise extensive use of the mine detectors and sniffer dogs in these projects. I wish to lay special emphasis on, take note, I am laying special stress on camp security. Besides ensuring well built morchas, we shall have to pay special care to access control. Surprise mobile parties must also dominate the area. Further, the intelligence sources in the local areas need to be developed through a proper, well worked out, talent search.

Our men have this common tendency to become laid back and overlook the mandatory security drills. As we all know, at any point, at any juncture, anytime, threat can loom large on the horizon. Our supervisory officers need to regularly interact with our men and eloquently voice their concern about such laxity. This needs to become second habit.

Then in any case, offence is the best form of defence. Therefore, tactical operations should be frequently launched to keep the enemy on tenterhooks and constantly on the run. Why allow them the opportunity to approach our camps and take us by surprise? Let us follow a reversal of our roles from now on! Keep them on the run, avoid allowing them breathing space and a chance to retaliate.

Now during the community interface programmes, we should undertake forceful propaganda against them. This I am inclined to agree. I think our intelligence branch should get down with it and prepare the required plan along with the detailed material being made available.

Debojit, paused for effect, passing a fleetingly piercing swift glance across the room at all its occupants who were by now vigorously nodding their heads in conformity. Realising that he had gained their approval, he resumed, "And lastly, I want our communication branch to install interceptors so that we may be able to intercept and record the relevant communication of the insurgents. I'm sure you are already aware of the fact that we have successfully gathered sufficient data to decipher their code language. The surrendered and the apprehended insurgents have also been compelled to decode their language. We also intend now to take up the matter with the government to grant us some developmental projects. And of course, one thing remains unchanged - we have to retain the public support in our favour at all costs. We need not be driven by the political forces when approaching the problems at hand. We have to, at all costs, maintain a professional approach. We have to ensure that we are able to thwart their attempts, otherwise we can forget about the insurgents coming to an amicable settlement with the government. That, I think, will be all for the day. Thanks for the very patient and earnest hearing. Let us now proceed for some lunch," ended Debojit extending a patronising look at all his subordinates. He was slowly beginning to feel a wee bit optimistic once again.

* * *

Chapter 9

THE DILEMMAS

Debojit was feeling heavily bogged down with his work and an increasing sense of responsibility. He was constantly busy planning the forthcoming operations and allocating duties to all the members of his team. The Government on the other end had sent out their invitations to the LF leaders to approach them for a round table settlement talk.

Suddenly, the orders were issued that the underground insurgents were to be allowed to surface and escorted safely for the 'talks'. There would be no arrests, no encounters.

Debojit, too, was given clear instructions to do the same. He had immediately reacted strongly, sending forth his protests that the insurgents should be first compelled to lay down their arms. But, his repeated pleas had fallen on deaf ears. The LF had also resisted his move on the grounds that if they first laid down arms and later the Government did not accede to their demands, they would lose their standing amongst their own people. In fact, they demanded unconditional talks. Even the pundits of plotting, the think tanks, had no counter to this declaration by the LF. Anyways, the drills were plainly laid down. LF declared the place where they would meet. They were insistent that their armed guards would accompany them for their safety and the Government security forces were to remain at bay. Finally, helpless and supportless, he had been left with no choice.

It was just two days away from the talks, Debojit's SOG teams were all out, galvanised on the move. He did not wish to call them back. Retrieval was out of question. The results were obvious. The operations continued unabated and a few members of the LF became their victims. A major furore ensued. The DGP was forced to intervene and bail out the forces. The solution - the District Police Chief, Debojit was transferred out. Heads needed to roll. The entire department had to face the brunt. The dilemma intensified. But one major outcome of Debojit's stance was that he became the new prime target of the LF. They were now out to get him and what could be more effective than to use his own wife, Charu to target him. This irony of fate! Life's twists and turns, they never fail to catch one off guard!

Today is the day the talks were to take place. The common men around the town waited with bated breath apprehensive of the backlash by the insurgents and the administration.

The press fraternity had already fanned out all around the Secretariat where the top leaders of the LF were to arrive. Many of them were new faces or those that had remained underground for so long that they were now the faces, quite forgotten and unknown. This had aroused the curiosity of both the present press and the public at large. They had thronged the permitted outskirts since the crack of dawn.

Very soon a huge fleet of vehicles, well escorted, with blaring sirens announced the arrival of the LF leaders. People freely feasted their eyes upon this dreaded vision that came escorted with their own guards and under really tight security. A quick clear passing glimpse and then the entire group disappeared behind the imposing Secretariat walls.

A scuffle ensued with a few over-enthusiastic, leading media personnel, scuttling around in an effort to break through the police cordon in order to get a clearer, longer and closer shot of the LF leaders.

The crowd continued to persist long after the leaders had disappeared within the secure walls of the secretariat. Curious onlookers and the media could be seen moving around the outskirts, anxious to learn about the transactions inside. All were worried, tense and even to a certain degree, curious. What would it lead to next?

The day gradually dragged on. The enthusiasm of the people still hanging in the periphery of the compound had gradually slackened. People could be seen, loitering along the walls aimlessly, sitting in small groups, lazing and stretching out on the well preserved surrounding lawns. Some slept blissfully unaware of the moving hours of the day.

Shadows gradually began to lengthen; the cloud cover seemed to be once again taking over the skies. The sun had lost its intense freshness and was slowly traversing the entire length of the skies moving towards its western nightly quarters. The day seemed to have stretched out long enough, it was successively appearing more and more tired, and was now drawing to a quiet close. So were the expressions, now surfacing on the faces of those who had waited patiently, persistently waited outside, they too had begun to look lost, almost forlorn.

Then the clock struck six in the evening. Suddenly, there was a marked increase in the activity level along the huge imposing corridors of the secretariat that seemed to stretch deep within the premises. The media had been approached. They were invited in for a joint press briefing. The media trooped in single file. Provision was also made for a live coverage with a display panel outside the secretariat on a huge screen. A live coverage was also arranged at various other strategic points of the town. The TV channels were also ready to give it a live coverage. What was displayed on the screen for the benefit of the public was the Chief Minister, all smiles, leading with the LF leaders on either side. They looked like the cat that had just licked the cream! A joint declaration was made – they had reached an amicable agreement to put an end to all armed struggle and to form an autonomous council which would be managed by the elected representatives. Anybody would have the right to contest for representation from given areas. Well, what a positive note, the whole drama seemed to be ending on! The media, of course, had sniffed the rat and were promptly ready with a volley of questions.

"Are you to deposit all your arms with the Government?" enquired a media representative.

"Yes, we would to the extent possible", came the prompt response from the LF spokesperson.

"Meaning thereby"?

"We shall conduct it in gradual phases as the accord is successfully implemented."

"What about the insurgents who are on the wanted list? Would they be surrendering?" another targeted the LF spokesperson.

"No, we do not rely on the police records. Moreover, we are now collectively going to take a fresh look", spoke the LF representative.

"Are the associated groups also opting for surrender?" persisted another media man.

"I'm afraid, not all! Some are resisting our move. We are still attempting to work out the modalities with them."

The Chief Minister could be seen becoming visibly discomfited by the constant digging out activities of the media on the scene. It was fast becoming apparent to all and sundry that the Government was playing to the dictates of the LF. The more the media pried, the more it was heating up the issue.

The Chief Minister, realising the delicacy of the issue, intervened. He abruptly cut off the media.

"We expect your cooperation in the matter. A more pragmatic approach would help. We will be issuing a white paper on the accord very soon with all the details", so saying, the CM arose along with the LF Chief to leave the media hall. Amidst innumerable camera flashes, the delegation briskly left the scene.

The white paper on the issue was released. The Government gave a package of Rs.500 crores to the council. It was granted all the powers for administrative decision making, including the transfer posting of the Government officials within the delineated areas of the council.

Certain villages were also handed over to the LF. They had been a continuous bone of contention and the Government had earlier been reluctant to give them to the council in view of the resistance from the other groups.

It was fast becoming obvious for all to see that the Government move would encourage seeds of dispute which could lead to volatile germination of anything, anytime in the future. Trouble was brewing. The Assam cauldron was now bubbling. Signals of an outburst were beginning to fester.

A few had read between the lines. They called it a carefully studied political move to create a rift between the councillors in the future. They declared that they would go on to use the other groups to create issues for the management of the autonomous council.

Anyhow the deal was struck!

Only time would tell the sagacity of the move. How the system would eventually work, was still not very clear. It had very visible loops within loops. The 'Accord' was also to pass successfully the litmus test of the Assembly where all the MLAs of the opposition were bound to use their magnifying lenses to indulge in severe nit picking, pin pointing the said drawbacks to their own political advantage.

However, they would not be doing this openly as they were not immune to the possible overbearing dark clouds of LF threats. The LF had already publicly declared that it was only open to its phased out implementation.

Now the council was to take a clear-cut shape. It was going to be a daunting task. Never an easy task to undertake, with the power game having its own sharp hitting, inbuilt frictions and ulterior strokes that had become a constant threat.

"The Chief is playing it safe, you know. He will not be coming to the fore. He is avoiding the limelight till things take a clearer picture. He is following the age old policy of 'wait and watch' first", Deka seemed distinctly disconcerted as he declared his concern to Charu about the intentions of Prodeep (*The Chief*).

"Hummmm......" was Charu's only studied reaction.

"You know, we will be required to fix our councillors from every ward. Elections would be required to make it appear honestly 'democratic' though, several places would find only one contestant, as determined by us", opined Deka.

"Are you truly so naïve so as to believe it to be a cakewalk? Our political wing may not be so forthcoming. Do not take their cooperation for granted. There is a distinct possibility that they may reflect a clear disinclination to involve the armed wing, except may be sparingly, just to put up a show that very few people have adopted the democratic bent. Anyway, so far you have got an assured slot all right", Charu retorted with a mischievous grin.

"Oh yeah! And you, too! And now for the clincher. Lucky for you, my dear. I have heard that Debojit is taking over as the Police Chief within the United Area Council i.e.UAC", smirked Deka.

"You are an incorrigible.......," Charu snorted, but letting better judgment take over, she immediately restrained her reactions.

Realising that he had probably overstepped his limits, Deka apologetically reassured, "I am sorry, that was uncalled for. I retract my words. Am I forgiven?"

"Yeah, just this once. But get one thing clear - I am not open to joining the council. No way! I think somebody here needs to keep our issue smouldering, our coals glowing till the picture firmly falls in place. Then, also at present we are in no situation to ascertain as to how far the Government really means business. We really can't trust them. Do you really think they are serious in their declarations? I can clearly see through their nefarious game plans. We haven't yet declared our intentions and they have already started making efforts to placate us with a Rs.500 crore package. Dangling the carrot before our noses, aren't they? They are very coyly baiting us. It is quite obvious, they realise that it would attract the opportunists to join the council," fumed Charu in disgust.

"Oh! I am in complete agreement with you. One can smell a rat. Things are truly threatening to get out of control. That's a master stroke they've played, and the unsuspecting are going to fall for it like nine pins. Things, sure, are getting a bit too complex here," came Deka's acceptance.

Charu had learnt her lessons well. She now had a lot of experience stowed away under her white hat. "If they think they are smart, they haven't seen our worst. We shall not under any cost let ourself be fooled into surrendering our vital weaponry and, of course, we shall also ensure the withdrawal of all the cases against our Johnnies", Charu was busy chalking out their counter plans and the desired course of action for them.

"Well, you couldn't be closer to the truth. You have unknowingly hit the bull's eye. I don't see how the Chief could not have figured this out. But, he seems to be taking his own sweet time making up his mind", Deka outlined his thoughts aloud.

"Whatever! My goal and decision is final. I know some views will never undergo a change. You can see for yourself that despite the 'accord', two of our area commanders have been shot dead in fake encounters. Does this not give out a message to us very loud and clear?" Charu now looked visibly upset.

Deka was an old hand at this game. He had long realised that it would be prudent on his part to ignore the issue. 'Look the other way', his inner self advised him. This was probably based on his experiences during his long tenure in this place. Then of course, he had his own personal plans. He could finally envision his long drawn out dream of taking over as the administrative head, turning into a reality. Now his eyes were focused only on the major chunk of the pie, all other issues be damned! He wisely slinked away, politely excusing himself.

Soon, he had left for an unknown destination.

However, it was not to remain a mystery for long. The decision was made and finally announced by their political wing. The structure along with the declared action plan of the UAC had been rejected. The following dawn brought with it a fresh list of candidates from the multiple districts and wards. Most of them obviously were Deka's blue eyed boys. It was now obvious for all to see that Deka was the new Head of the UAC.

Amidst the heart of all this hubub and action there was one man quietly brooding over the developments, Debojit, as he was now going to have to work under the likes of Deka. It had been unimaginable, the least of all the possibilities, and yet ironically fate had delivered the hard blow and decided just that for him. Debojit was beginning to feel asphyxiated; he was increasingly finding it difficult to breathe. The frustration was gradually turning into a festering carbuncle readying to burst and drain! In the isolation of his quarters, Debojit poured himself another stiff peg of whiskey. The air inside the room was as dark, bleak and oppressive as the humid, dark, unfriendly weather outside. Swimming deep in a whirlpool of latent anger, his thoughts took gradual flight, they moved on from a vision of the abhorring Deka to his next in command – Charu!

Debojit could feel the heat becoming unbearable inside him, his insides were singeing in the flames of hostility and frustration. His eyes had turned crimson, the fine capillaries swelling into an angry red. His fingers gripped the bottom of the glass. The grasp tightened.

There came a sharp sound of shattering glass. Fine splinters forced their way into the crevices of his roughened palm. Slowly, very slowly, bright red, angry spots appeared on his hand oozing till they dripped forming a small puddle on the cold, helpless floor.

His voice boomed through the empty melancholy of the room, "...........you bitch!"

* * *

Chapter 10

FREEDOM

The days flew past; the working systems that had undergone drastic changes were gradually being accepted. The master stroke players had assumed the saddle as planned. But the shadows of the old towering bamboos continued to stretch on. They were once again gradually taking root within restless bellies, slowly taking a firm hold and still growing. The bellies now bulged and had begun to assume threatening postures. Finally came the master move from that unsuspected quarter. She had always meant business. She hadn't bitched, she hadn't uttered a reproaching word, and no reaction had come from her so far. But she had made her decision- no more dilly dallying. Only action. She meant to retaliate!

She kept sending out the signals – a group of the LF had split and was still in exile. Deka was now the medium. She was now cleverly exploiting the present situation. She was ruthlessly compelling and pestering Debojit to go after them in a frantic attempt to nab them. She was a sharp learner and she had, gradually through successive years on the unfriendly trail, mastered all the crafty strokes popularly employed in their line that is, she was successfully using her own kingpin as informers to guide Debojit's moves and approaches.

"My heartiest congratulations to you. You've finally succeeded in nabbing and killing two very influential members of our split away group; they were a potential threat to our well being", Deka commented;

"Sir, we are trying our level best", saluted the unsuspecting Debojit.

"I hope the latest informers have proved to be lucrative to our cause. Have they supplied substantial information?", queried Deka with a carefully assumed anxious expression that spread across his features.

"Yes, all our movements lately and the success of the last operation were based on the inputs we'd received from them. They appear to be an earnest duo and have provided us with some vital information about their intended movements and whereabouts", elaborated a beaming Debojit.

A deceptively benign smile spread across Deka's harsh facial features "Good going, keep up the good work, Lieutenant.."

Debojit returned to his workplace and called for his second-in-command.

"Roy, any latest update?"

"No Sir, not yet. I did though go to meet the 'asset'?

"What is the latest from his quarters?"

"Very frankly sir, I have very serious doubts about the sincerity of his intent. It makes me wonder whether we are being wise in relying on him," Roy declared his concern.

"Why would you say so? Hasn't he proven his mettle and fair intent in two vital issues? Both the times we have made very successful overtures and returned with rich dividends, haven't we?" reacted an impatient Debojit.

"Sir, it is difficult to pinpoint what it is that bothers me about him. May be its just a gut feeling. But, I somehow can't bring myself to trust him. Lately, on several occasions in passing I've noticed that he seems to be hobnobbing a lot with those around you. I feel we need to get rid of him now. Forgive me if I should be overstepping, but my intuition tells me this very strongly, sir."

"I see your point, but it may annoy Deka," commented a subdued Debojit. "I wonder whether it would be wise to openly oppose his directions. It might have some serious repercussions if we rub Deka the wrong way you know. We need to consider the options carefully. A rash reaction may not help matters much, I really don't know.....,"trailed off an uncertain Debojit.

"Yes, there is the strong possibility that he may not reveal his reactions immediately. But then, knowing Deka, the bloody swine that he is, very frankly he may target us later, and move us to the lower operational grounds", continued Debojit after a few minutes of serious pondering.

"So in that case, I suggest, let us continue with him. If he should provide any fresh inputs, we shall send our teams to the said spot, if not, it is his head that cracks anyways", Debojit had reached a decision.

"Whatever you may say sir, you are the boss here. Yet, I will still reiterate, I'm not comfortable with this man, being here in such close proximity to you. After all, he does owe his final allegiance to Deka. Sir, please do reconsider", petitioned Roy.

Days rolled past, nothing had changed, until, one fine day – a message was flashed across all the wireless connections –

"Police Chief, Debojit, attacked in his office. Injuries prove to be fatal, he has succumbed to them."

Panic ensued. Everybody rushed to the site. A red alert was declared across the township. All exit points were blocked, security tightened.

The entire administration was unnerved. This was most unexpected.

What had really happened? What had transpired? No idea! Was it possible? Mr. Debojit killed, impossible! How did it come to be? The entire force was agog with questions. Attacked by insurgents? What was the guard doing at that moment? He has been killed as well! What! Everybody was perturbed. Nobody is safe in these times. God help us!

It was still not clear how it had transpired. The investigation teams were galvanised into action. The bodies lifted for postmortems and the bullets retrieved were from an A.K.-47. This was evident by the recovered empty cartridges from the scene of the crime.

"Shocking! Somebody had obviously done their homework well. It was a swift operation with a very slick modus operandi", declared the new Chief, Deepanker, who had taken over after Debojit's demise.

"Sir, I am afraid, it is not surprising", announced Roy for all to hear.

"Have you figured out the details?", queried the Chief.

"Yes sir, we've recovered another body in the vicinity, today in the morning", informed Roy.

"Why have I not been informed so far?" Deepanker now seemed visibly annoyed.

"I was about to update you on it, sir. The case now stands crystal clear. The body belongs to the informer, who was working with Mr. Debojit. Another AK-47 has also been recovered. The one used for the gruesome murder".

"Which murder?"

"Interestingly sir, all the three, Mr. Debojit, his guard and their informer were all shot down by the same AK-47"

"So, a common murderer, heh!"

"Sorry Sir, you're wrong, two miscreants have used the same weapon to kill, it is a gun officially issued to Debojit's gunner!"

"Hey! You've confused me now. You've just contradicted yourself".

"Sir, please, I need a patient hearing. I can visualise how it all happened and I think I have the evidence too. Hear me out, sir."

"Yes, go ahead. Elaborate your deductions please", nodded the new Chief, his curiosity aroused. He quickly wanted to get to the crux of the matter and then close the chapter. Bygones should best be bygones.

"Sir, this so called 'asset'-the informer, was Deka's man. Initially, he had come up with useful tips repeatedly on a couple of occasions, leading to the success of our operations. This obviously won him the complete confidence and acceptance of the erstwhile Chief, Mr. Debojit. Despite, my repeated warnings, the man had successfully wormed his way into Mr. Debojit's privy ear, so all my warnings fell upon deaf ears. The man had been seen frequently pow-wowing with Mr. Debojit's gunner. Their growing camaraderie was fast becoming evident for all to see. I really can't pinpoint why, but my hackles had been up for sometime-may be you could call it plain and simple intuition. But Mr. Debojit refused to even entertain any doubts on the matter.

Yesterday, as was by now very common, the man had visited Mr. Debojit's gunner and had casually in the course of their conversation, learnt about the working of the AK-47. Unsuspectingly the gunner had handed him the AK-47. The man then shot the gunner down and immediately rushed into Debojit's office. Gun shots reverberated across the corridor that lead to the office. Debojit's body was flayed with bullets and he slowly slumped to the floor. The miscreant, the operation having been accomplished, must have jumped out of the window and escaped."

"How did you draw this conclusion, Roy?"

"Simple sir, I merely put two and two together. Today after the informer's mutilated body was recovered, the Commander of the guards finally confessed that he had seen a hazy figure jumping out of the bosses window as the guard was rushing towards the corridor yesterday on hearing the gunshots."

"Why the hell, did he not inform right then?" queried a visibly perturbed Deepanker.

"Now, that is the other angle to the story. The man deserves to be suitably punished. Why he did not choose to respond is ambiguous, as he has given no convincing reasons for his insubordination.

As seems apparent, the informer after committing the murder, left the site of the crime, headed towards the jungle and there he is believed to have been intercepted by his killer, who obviously used the same murder weapon and abandoning it there along with the informer's body, disappeared", Roy further elaborated.

"A clear picture seems to be evolving now. Obviously things are not as straight forward. This seems to be a precursor of an apparent threat of a much greater magnitude," Deepanker announced his worried thoughts aloud.

"Exactly sir, I am now dead sure that it was one of Deka's men only, who has killed the informer and then carefully removed any possible prima facie evidence. The informer, now it appears as it is, was Deka's implant amidst us. May be Deka carried all along some old personal scores to settle as well,".

"I have been informed that Mr. Debojit's wife, Charu, also works with the insurgents and in fact she forms a core ingredient of Deka's group", Deepanker wanted a clear confirmation on this striking data that he had very recently come across.

"Oh, yes! Sir, that's another dimension that needs our careful probing into", reasserted Roy.

"Isn't that common knowledge?"

"No sir, not just that. But then could she be, may be she herself is the driving force behind Mr. Debojit's murder."

"Can we adduce any positive evidence? If you see the possibilities, you had better look into it then."

"Not at all impossible, sir. The ballistic reports along with the postmortem analysis say it all. Now what we need to work upon is to define and locate a strong link with the conspirators. We will not make any headway till we have managed to identify the man, the killer of the informer. There lies our vital link, our kingpin."

"A man? But why not look for a woman?", pearls of wisdom had casually dropped from the new chief.

"Ah......ha Charu Sir", and lightning had struck home.

"Yes, you do have the fingerprints on the weapon, don't you? Have them analysed carefully. Charu's prints may already be there in our records. Match them, if they are the same."

Somewhere in the hollows of his heart, Roy did not want to have to do this. Something inside him resisted believing in this possibility. Charu would not murder her Debojit. She couldn't, it almost seemed preposterous!

Deepanker emphatically issued the orders. Soon came the reports of the finger prints analysis.

"Yes, what is the outcome?"

"Sir, one of the print matches."

"Sure"

"Absolutely Sir."

"Do we need to carry out a recheck?"

"There is no need, sir!", muttered Roy, still downcast and visibly shaken. Was it possible? How could she? They had seen good times together, shared simple jokes, life's ups and downs, and faced life's adversities side by side. Whatever may have been the final outcome, they had still been husband and wife. Roy felt clueless. He watched on helpless to the fast evolving picture. Could a wife go down to such limits? Would not her conscience prick her, would not her hand shake at the prospect? Roy was crest-fallen. His belief in man had taken a severe battering.

Charu was a driven soul, burning up. Her insides were engulfed with the consuming flames of revenge. She knew no respite; she was a creature pushing to quench her thirst for revenge. Remorse, sanity, moderation, emotions found no place in her, so then what husband? The thought did not even for a brief moment faze her decision. Debojit deserved to die, she had to do it, she had to do it herself and she had done it!!

But now that he was gone! What now! She felt a slow vacuum building up within her. It was beginning to eat away her insides slowly, gradually. The woman in her, after years, was forcing its way up unrestrained. She had to fight off her surfacing deluge of emotions.

Debojit was to be cremated today with all the due state honours. He had died a hero on duty. Should she go, at least for the last rites? She owed it to him, did she not? Indecisive, she dilly dallied. The clocks arms moved slowly on. Soon, the chime struck five. And, the shrill telephone bell cut sharply upon the silence.

"Ma'am the cremation is over!"

The churning, uncontrolled whirlpool suddenly jolted to a halt. Pin drop silence!

Then, very slowly, the watery grave of emotions experienced another stir after years of a studied dull. The bandh finally collapsed and tears began to form in her eyes.....drop after drop they rolled down her dry, chapped cheeks. The day finally drew to a mourning close as the sun gradually crossed over to the western horizons to find its resting abode.

The threatening shadows of the bamboo shoots seemingly disappeared But, the deep waters of the Brahmaputra still carried the Silhouette.

* * *

Part–II

Fragments

Chapter 11

ENCOUNTER

It is a generally accepted norm that whenever the local police has found itself in a predicament, where it finds it difficult to cope with a given law and order imbroglio, forces from outside are drawn in to tackle the situation and restore peace and quiet in the area once again.

Assam has been one such troubled state. It has been an area that has had a history of a very long drawn out insurgency where the diverse groups have been demanding and fighting for autonomy of state and sovereignty in their own respective strongholds. As a consequence, the central forces have been deployed here since a long time.

There is no denying that low intensity war situations are very different from a direct war scenario where war is waged openly across the border. Here, one needs an altogether different level of acumen, dexterity and tackling prowess to systematically trace the miscreants and then successfully nab them at the opportune moment, all the while keeping within the legal boundaries. Here, one needs to keep a keen watch on the issues of collateral damage as well as the human rights involved in dealing with the crisis. Where as, on the other hand, there is an unrelenting constant pressure on the forces – the threat of a statistical evaluation of their performance in terms of the number of successful liquidations, arrests and recoveries that hang on their heads, waiting to fall like the sword of 'Damocles', if they should fail to meet the declared numbers.

The term 'family' stands for security and unity. On the other hand, here are men in these forces sent on long drawn out deployments in alien lands, leaving behind the security of their homes, distanced for long spells from their kith and kin, all alone in strange, unfriendly, unwelcome surroundings. Somewhere, in the deep recesses of their minds they are bound to gradually nurture a sense of emotional barrenness, insecurity and frustrations. Thus, this in turn, gives rise to a spectrum of other, sometimes ill founded, apprehensions that affect the response and efficacy of the forces.

One such battalion of the anti-insurgency force of the Central Government was deployed in a location which was a stone's throw away, from the district headquarters of Barpeta, in Assam. This was a medium sized district located in the lower stretches of Assam where a majority of the population still depended upon agriculture. There, farming that was carried out on small fragmented pieces of land was still the main source of filling up their bellies. It was a case of high costs and very low returns. Even the mode of farming was very primitive. Not only that, a sizeable chunk of the community survived merely on the weeds that were rampant in the stale waters of the ponds and the back waters of that area. A starving, deprived community fell easy prey to the carrot dreams waved before them. Particularly, their youth eagerly succumbed to the option of toting and brandishing a gun and joining the insurgents in exchange for the dream comforts of a fascinating lifestyle. They were easy prey to the allure of these offered comforts, as against the misery, hunger, humiliation and fear psychosis inflicted upon them by the then ruling government and the forces notwithstanding.

Amit, a young enterprising officer had only recently taken up the command of this battalion, which had shifted to Barpeta. He was raring to go, enthusiastic and still wrapped in the dreams of an ideal. So, he had been insisting 'on exceptional work outcomes' from his subordinates. Moreover, he had to sign the monthly performance records that were regularly forwarded to his superiors. For the last two months in succession he had been signing 'nil' returns. Luckily, an initial 'wait and watch' period of two months was allowed to an officer to give him time to settle down and familiarise himself with the place and its people. But what now? Amit was getting frantic, in fact he had begun to panic. He had conducted long drawn out meeting sessions with his second-in-command, Rakesh. Rakesh, though his subordinate, was far senior in years. He was a science graduate, more seasoned, realistic and systematic in his approach. He did not approve of following the dictates of 'rushing in a hurry and then repenting in leisure'. He was well aware that the lands were still foreign to them and the strength, hideouts of the enemy unknown to them. In other words, the potential threat that loomed large in the form of an unfamiliar enemy was still not successfully assessed.

Yet on being repeatedly reprimanded by his boss he had activated his sources to net some 'catch'. And as luck would have it, on the very third day, Rakesh received a message, an urgent update, from his 'source' – one of the insurgents from their middle order was likely to visit the crowded market place in the early hours of the evening. He even gave the details of the shops he was most likely to visit. The source identified this insurgent as 'GOPANG'. The source refused to jeopardize his safety further by coming out in the open. Instead, he provided details of another man who would point out the 'victim' from a discreet distance, sitting in a vehicle, positioned safely and at the same time allowing him a clear overview of the shop in question.

The effort bore fruit and Gopang was identified and arrested. He turned out to be a twenty-three years old young, fit, educated yet unemployed youth.

Without much resistance, he candidly confessed having been an associate of the insurgents in that area. But in the same breath he declared however that he had had no further dealings with them for sometime and was now trying to find his grove back in society and to leading a normal life. He willingly offered to them all the information that he carried – he told them whatever he knew, the details of their training camps, their modus operandi, their locales and their carefully chosen hideouts. He also gave a detailed honest update of all their activities along with the 'sources' through which the truth of his claims could be verified.

The local police in the meanwhile had also joined in the operation. One of them, Deputy Suptt. of Police carrying the surname of 'Bohra', had sent his folks and got the details verified. The man spoke the 'truth! The constables on the daily beat confirmed that, though earlier associated with the insurgents, Gopang was trying hard to reallocate himself into a straight forward lifestyle and a nine to five desk job. He was clearly on the 'come back' trail.

However, life has this silly way of playing a spoilt sport! Just when things seemed to be looking up for Gopang, it decided to intercept and bring it to a grinding halt. The overzealous top cops present, during his interrogations decided to play 'God'. They did not relish the idea of Gopang being released and left again to join the mainstream of humanity. Infact, quick to sense the mood of their senior, very discreetly 'a gun' that would later be claimed to be in the possession of the unsuspecting Gopang was arranged to make the case of the seniors stronger.

In the meanwhile, more complications were to set in, furthering Gopang's destiny. One of Amit's troops that had gone to conduct an area operation in the vicinity of the Nalbari forest was ambushed by an insurgent group active in that area. Unfortunately for Gopang, one of the constables in the troop, badly hit by the bullets, immediately succumbed to his injuries.

Amit, learning of the mishap, rushed to the spot following a shorter route through the jungle paths guided by the local DSP, Mr. Barua who also happened to be present there with Amit.

Despite cutting down the distance travelled considerably, the difficult, unfriendly forested path still ate up a little over two hours before they arrived at the spot. The exchange of fire had stopped on both the sides. The air had a strange quiet. The insurgents seemed to have receded for the time being.

The dead body of the constable had been lifted into one of the standing vehicles.

The surrounding area gave a tired and desolate feel. It threatened to be a dark night with the sun receding to its resting quarters and the moon appearing to have decided to skip its beat for the night.

Amit slowly assessed the situation. It seemed to indicate dark tidings for them. The outcome did not look optimistic at all. Far from it, his men had fired seven hundred and forty rounds, without killing any insurgent. On the contrary, they had lost a soldier. No, the future appeared bleak to him. He could already visualise himself standing before his superiors with his head sunk in shame, down cast eyes appraising the ground while they blasted him with a volley of questions, counter questions and reprimands. Yes, a chastening process was going to be due now, and for the present, he could see no escaping from it. He stood there crestfallen!

He had put up a pathetic show of commandeering and he knew it!

Slowly, pulling himself together he began a detailed reassessment of the situation with Bohra, carefully considering its pros and its cons. Bit by bit, they went through the unfortunate mishap and the 'face-saving' possibilities that they might still have.

Suddenly, out of the blue, Bohra's excited voice, his eyes gleaming with an evil glint of glee announced "I have it sir, I have just what we need to do! We need to get Gopang here and knock him off right here! That's it sir! Then we can say, Yes! We lost one of our soldiers but we killed one of their men, too!"

A stunned Amit stood without reacting for a good few seconds before he could barely murmur, "Would that be proper?"

"Why the hell not sir?" reacted an enthralled Bohra. Realising his reaction was unprecedented, Bohra softened his stance. He continued, "We could show a joint operation. The local police will support you on this. We shall also carefully erase all the recent incriminating evidence in his history, in our records, that may prove that he was on the way to reforming and no longer was a vital link in the chain of the insurgents' group. Sir, not just your force, but we shall also reap the benefits of this act, you see now for quite sometime we have not had any encounters. My chief would be ecstatic too", Bohra was barely able to suppress a vicious giggle.

Still apprehensive, Amit enquired, "How shall we go about it, hiding the possible evidences?"

"Sir, leave it to us. You need not worry your head regarding the details. Consider them already taken care of. I shall instruct my SHO to carefully have every remanent of blackening or charring evidence on Gopang's body avoided. The killing will be a neat job. He will also handle the inquest and the postmortem report details", elaborated Barua.

Carefully considering the solution offered by Barua, Amit still felt a wee bit queasy on making the call on his own. He decided to take the advice of his second-in-command Rakesh before giving his approval. He voiced his concern before Barua.

Barua's typical careless reaction was, "Oh you can talk to him over the phone from our office itself. It's barely half a kilometer away from this spot."

Amit was still not comfortable with this policy though it was slowly dawning upon him that there really was no other way out. If he wanted to escape being at the receiving end of the wrath of his superiors, he would have to carry this 'cross' along too.

Still wary and confused Amit inquired, " I hope your phones are not tapped?"

"That is why I am asking you to use our Chowki phone and not a PCO", obviously Barua had already decided that the matter had been settled. He directed a sharp look at the nearby standing SHO and his eyes clearly directed the SHO to accompany Amit along to the Chowki.

It was not going to be easy for Amit to convince his second-in-command.

In the meantime, Amit too had now set the ball rolling on his end. He had forwarded the message on his radio set. It recorded that a dangerous miscreant going by the name of Gopang had been arrested. He had been caught carrying a weapon with him.

Rakesh was an extremely disturbed man. He was a man of moderate ambitions. He did not believe in taking risks and pursuing the short cut to success. And above all, his conscience did not permit him to become party to taking away somebody's life like this, just to further their own interests. No way, he could not agree. "Sir", Rakesh declared, "Let us not fall in this trap. Let us report the happenings just as they have taken place. After all, we cannot be responsible for the action or the inaction of others. But, we do have a responsibility to ourselves. We do need to know what it is that we are doing. Sir, we really should not even be considering this other option. At the risk of sounding rude, I will state, that if we do so, we may live to rue it on another day", a visibly agitated Rakesh was making no bones regarding his disapproval on his boss's stance regarding the matter on hand.

Amit could feel his confidence crumbling. Rakesh was forcing him to reconsider. Should they, should they not? He felt perplexed, he could feel his blood gushing to his temples making them throb. However, he still gave orders to Rakesh to get Gopang to the spot and by that time he would decide what was to be done.

Putting the receiver of the phone back on its pedestal, Amit let escape a deep sigh. He felt weighed down, pulled in two divergent directions – his good sense beckoned him towards the more practical step while his conscience told him otherwise. Moving in a daze, he reached the adjoining room where Barua was waiting for him with tea already served on the glass table, standing in the Centre.

Still feeling disgusted, yet finding his hands tied, Rakesh arrived on the spot with Gopang. Giving it his last desperate attempt to prevent his boss from going ahead with his plan Rakesh pointed out that he had already relayed the message of Gopang's arrest on the wireless and, therefore, it was not possible to declare him killed now.

Barua, an old hat at these games, irritably chipped in, "That is hardly an issue. We shall declare that after having arrested Gopang we were bringing him here, for showing us their hideouts, when we were intercepted by his fellow insurgents. Taking advantage of the distraction Gopang attempted to sneak out of our clutches to join his friends. He was then killed in the crossfire. Simple!" Then standing up, without waiting for a reaction from Amit, Barua left them with the carelessly thrown in comment "Okay! That's decided. Let me get down to business while you guys make up your minds. We need to interrogate the man thoroughly. Let me get my inspector to get on the job. Meanwhile, you may send your inspector to join him too."

Amit immediately responded, directing his Inspector to do the needful. The interrogating team got down to dissecting the poor, unsuspecting Gopang.

Shortly, followed another tea session. Rakesh made a fresh effort to convince those that surrounded him.

"Surprisingly, Gopang seems to be a well educated man. He could prove to be an asset if given a chance. Obviously, the man had been gravely misled by the insurgents. Otherwise, I can sense the potential in him, if given the right start and guidance. It would be inhuman on our part to take this chance away from him. He has old ailing parents and a young still to be married sister at home. They are his responsibility. He is their soul bread earner. We can't snatch that away from them. And, particularly now when he is promising to reform, we cannot take that away from them. Our God above shall question the prudence of our decision, if we do not give him this chance. We are all God fearing men here, please sir, do not get carried away in the heat of the moment. Think again, I beseech you ….."

Rakesh's words were left incomplete as the local police SHO entered and declared "Saab – kam to ho gaya (Sir, the work is done)". Rakesh continued to persist, "We could have just handed him over to the local police and not kill him in the encounter."

"Enough, what's done is done. Now, there is no going back on your words. Did you not hear what my SHO just said? And mind you, you had your own Inspector working on him too", an offended Barua thundered.

They all got up and followed Barua to where Gopang's body was lying. Gopang ....the poor fellow who never even had the faintest inkling that all this drama, this last interrogation, had actually been a formal declaration of his death warrant.

"Don't worry, you have been a great help. I shall positively recommend your case for an award," Amit patted Rakesh, not meeting his eyes, But his mind was now made up.

Rakesh could feel the nausea building up within him. These were truly 'the wretched of the wretch' and he was actually abetting their cause. How low they had fallen! His insides screamed for rebellion but his facial contours took on a sheepish look as his resolve weakened. His voice of revolt had managed to rise to the gullet but then it felt forced to subside.

He could hear those around sniggering, openly ridiculing his 'immaturity' that is what they were calling his 'principles'.

And above it all, he heard the loud clear voice of Amit, his boss reporting to his seniors, "Sir, this is to report, we have killed one insurgent and made substantial recoveries. One of our jawans too has sacrificed his life. He is a martyr".

Next day was followed by several rounds of applause. Amit and his men had done a commendable job. They were the heroes of the hour.

But somewhere within Amit, something continued to simmer, something that was gradually burning up his soul, eating away his insides with a nagging guilt of repeated reminders that he had done wrong. He did not deserve the praise! That day it had not been the encounter of 'Gopang', the insurgent alone, somewhere Amit had killed his conscience too in that very operation!

* * *

Chapter 12

OPERATION 'CATS'

'Avinash the undefeatable' is how he had come to be addressed. This was a name that was dreaded both in the police circles and amongst the insurgents alike. Within a short period of 'five years' he had had over fifty successful encounters to his credit. He was an able Commandant, gifted with exceptional resourcefulness and a shrewd foresight. He had amply proved his mettle with his amazingly dexterous police operations that had become the popular topic of discussion over tea even amongst the common folks. His colleagues envied his resourcefulness. What could be the secret behind his quick and accurate information? What were his sources? These questions perplexed his colleagues and his enemies alike. It was probably easier to conduct an operation but to successfully extract accurate details was what entailed exceptional expertise and prowess.

The other frustrated officers envied his success, as they were often quoted as the typical standing examples of "all dressed up but nowhere to go".

Of course, exceptional success entails exceptional means, so Avinash too had gradually learnt smart ways of 'flouting the rules'. His seniors, however, tolerated him and his questionable means only because of his success rate. Avinash was a highly decorated police officer. He would use local vehicles, local people, local arenas, soldiers attired in local dress to make surprise attacks on the enemy. The insurgents actually knew no peace now. They were constantly on tenterhooks as they were under a constant threat of surprise attacks.

It was the early hours of an unusually chilly morning when the news flashed across the police wireless –

'A police gypsy no.7342 along with two private cars, carrying the police monogram have been detained by the customs officials as they were intercepted carrying sixteen packets of heroin, which were obviously being smuggled out. However, the involved police party is absconding.'

Avinash had already taken command of the situation. He had had prior notice of the possibilities and was already monitoring the incident. He had been informed on the previous night by his sub-inspector Mohan Kumar, the man who had been commanding the convoy of the three vehicles in which the 'herion' had been discovered. However, this time the poor man had been taken completely unawares. He had no inkling that his vehicles were carrying such contraband drugs. He was a completely shattered man when he had made the frantic call to his senior. He had appeared visibly shaken. Avinash had immediately assessed the possibilities and carefully barked out the necessary directions to his junior. He was a master strategist and his mind went on overdrive, analysing the future course of action. He told his man to lie low. He then patiently waited for the announcement to be made on the wireless.

As soon as he received the written message he issued formal orders of a search notice against Mohan Kumar and the remaining absconding cops. As instructed by Avinash, these men had fled as soon as the customs officers apprehended the vehicles carrying the drugs. Avinash also issued orders for an internal enquiry to be conducted. At the same time, he initiated a brief report that was forwarded to his Seniors with the assurance that a report of the detailed findings would follow at the earliest.

The very next day, early morning he himself travelled to Karbi-anglong, a location about eight kilometers from his headquarters.

There, he slyly stage managed the arrest of Mohan Kumar as per their earlier agreed plan. Thereafter Mohan Kumar gave the statement as smartly tutored by his boss, Avinash. Avinash had carefully manoeuvred his lines managing to keep himself totally in the clear.

The story that Mohan had to give was that he had been on a hot trail of a few suspected insurgents. In the bargain, they had picked up some characters enroute on the basis of suspicion. It could have been a ploy by somebody envious of their success. He claimed that he had no idea how those 'packets' had come to be loaded in his vehicles and where actually they had been placed in his vehicle.

Mohan was obviously nervous, Avinash on this pretext had a few specific medicines administered to Mohan that they would help ease his nerves. Then, as tutored, gradually over the course of 3-5 days the unit doctor treating Mohan declared that he needed to be referred to a 'psychiatric specialist' for further treatment. Gradually, Mohan was declared mentally unfit to serve any further and dismissed from service.

The remaining troopers involved in this incident were also soon tracked down and brought to the unit. Here, carefully structured and stage managed statements were taken down from them. Very soon, the whole episode was coloured to project that the sole villain in this whole incident was none other than Mohan himself. But then, there is a God, who has his own unique ways of passing judgement. Avinash had successfully declared Mohan the sole culprit in this front. But, he was flummoxed on another front.

There was a parallel system that he had been running from one of his units. But lately he had been losing control over them. He had, therefore, failed to keep them in careful check. Due to some heavy exchange of fire between the inmates of this camp, it was brought to everybody's notice. These inmates were actually the Commandant Avinash's hidden "assets", his main backbone, and the reason behind his stupendous performance and results.

They were a group that functioned independently, and were beyond any control. There were clear cut instructions that nobody dare curb their movements, no one dare to track where or when they came or went.

But now Avinash was forced to intervene. He reached the camp to control the indiscipline and settle the dispute amongst them. The dispute was a consequence of the resultant loss that the inmates had suffered owing to the seizure of the 'heroin' consignment by the Customs. They had also become suspicious of each other. Each was questioning the loyalty of the other, as each felt that the other was responsible for leaking the information about the consignment to the customs authorities.

Everything comes at a cost. Avinash was well aware that the 'group', though an invaluable asset for him with regard to the success of his operations conducted against the insurgent groups, was not above board in their own dealings. He had, however, chosen to turn the 'Nelson's eye' with regard to their spurious underhand dealings as the cost involved could be very high. He was an ambitious man and over the years he had won the image of the 'invincible cop' but it was not without a cost. He knew that this 'network of men' that he had nurtured over the years were substantially responsible for his success. Without them, he could return to being a 'naught'. He needed them desperately to successfully implement his strategic winnings against the sprawling network of insurgents in that area. He needed them enough to turn a blind eye to their greed and growing avarice.

But then good tidings never last forever. Just as good news travels fast, bad news spreads even faster. There was now a fast spreading gossip that was taking firm route in the 'Langar gazette' of the force about some group of dreaded insurgents, termed as 'CATS', that were being nurtured by their present Commandant. The word went around that these 'CATS' fed the Commandant with the latest whereabouts, the strength, movements and the modus operandi of the insurgents and that is how he carried out and succeeded in his 'operations'.

These 'CATS' were also fast gaining the reputation of being active in smuggling and it was said that Avinash too was benefitting from their dealings. Thus, slowly his immaculate reputation was beginning to take a beating.

Consequently, his good dealings, his liberal doses of doling out money for the comforts of his troops were now given a fresh corrupt twist. This finally triggered off an enquiry that was ordered by his seniors to look into the operational conduct of the Commandant, Avinash and his so called 'associates'.

Pushed with his back against the wall, Avinash now felt compelled to get rid of the 'CATS'. He had now become desperate to springclean his tarnished image. In his desperation he ordered some of his trusted juniors to 'bump off' two of the so called 'CATS'. His instructions were implemented immediately that very night, at a little distance from the location. This was not really 'uncommon' amongst them. It often happened that once a vital link became a possible threat to the top brass, he was knocked off, as his staying alive would prove to be a greater threat to their well being.

However, what Avinash had not known was that the 'CATS' were somehow linked to the local MLA, who had a lot of clout in the area. Now he realised that he needed to wipe off systematically the whole group of the 'CATS' or else, he would be finished. Avinash was fast becoming hysterical. He sensed the threat closing in on him. So, every member of this carefully garnered group was now exterminated.

The MLA was livid. The row between Avinash and the MLA intensified.

Then, after a lapse of three days, the MLA met with a serious car accident and succumbed to his injuries on the spot. How it had happened, and why, was anybody's guess! The wild stories carried by the 'Langar Gagette' intensified further. Avinash became a scary figure. A dreaded man!

The seniors finally realised that Avinash had become too big for his boots. And he needed his wings to be substantially clipped. There were no options left. Avinash had to be suspended now.

Once a man is out of power, the tide misses no time in taking a double turn. And so, the tide now turned against poor Avinash, a man once a force to contend with was now a man without any friends! Nobody wanted to touch him with a barge pole!

D.P. Singh, the Inspector General of Police, carefully went about with his enquiries. The statements now recorded had an altogether different story to tell than the reports submitted earlier. The picture had taken a complete hundred and eighty degree turn.

The earlier statement and details submitted by Avinash of all his subordinate staff were in total consonance with the rules and regulations. For instance, the motor transport incharge had earlier narrated that all the vehicles had been carefully and thoroughly checked on that morning of the 'heroin' episode. Nothing had been found out of line.

Similarly, the duty incharge had given a list of the police party that had boarded the vehicles and the items that were carried by them. It stated that they had been carefully checked after they had been briefed for their respective duties. It specified that there had been no outsiders in the team. The gates of the camp also had corresponding entries of the check outs of the respective vehicles along with the indicated team. Hence, it was clearly stated in the report that the vehicles on venturing out from the camp had been found to be clear with nothing planted in them.

This earlier report of the internal enquiry was subjected to lot of fresh grilling by the present IG, D.P. Singh. The subordinate staff could not stand up to his smart, wily and witty repartee and soon succumbed confessing the truth.

Then, of course, it is always difficult to create a fool hardy documentation, particularly if it lacks integrity and if it is falsely initiated.

Mr. D.P. Singh was quick to track the inconsistencies and the contradictions with a flourish. The poor sub-inspector Balvinder, the officer incharge of the motor transport, keeled under his pressure tactics and confessed.

Singh now had in his hold clear confessions that the said vehicles had never reported to camp, so they had not been frisked. Infact, even their log books had been filled in later, in one go, after a gap of almost six months. They had reportedly been busy in some operations and so had not touched base. Once, this was determined, it was now child's play for Singh to ascertain that there were considerable flaws in the duty roster too. Thus, it was established that certain members of the staff never reported back to the lines. They had in fact been seen hobnobbing with the so called 'CATS' of the Commandant Avinash, the touch me nots, whose activities and movements were never cross-questioned.

In fact, the truth soon spilled out that these members of the 'Police staff' had in fact been handsomely rewarded, some even awarded rank promotions. They had fast grown to become the star components of that unit.

They had come to wield unchecked authority amongst the junior rungs always having the unflinching support of Avinash.

Having tasted success, Singh delved deeper into the issues. Now he went about meticulously tracking down all the then involved staff, sitting with them individually, conducting long gruelling session of cross examination till the actual chain of events started to emerge. Particularly Mohan proved to be the most lucrative source to Singh. He was a wronged man, who had suffered deeply for no fault of his own. He had been a mere pawn who had been ruthlessly exploited by Avinash in his shrewdly evolved game of chess. The poor fellow had been dismissed from service on charges of 'mental disorder'. He had been at the receiving end of the brunt of Avinash's unscrupulous game. He was a man waiting to pounce and now he did! The ugly truth came pouring out with an intensity that took even Singh by surprise.

The truth was now out!

The police party that had been intercepted by the customs officers had constituted of the 'CATS' whose frisking had never taken place earlier in the police camp. They carried with them whatever they desired. They stopped whenever they needed enroute, to do whatever they wanted in the name of the 'Police Operation', unquestioned as they travelled in uniform and in the police vehicles.

These 'CATS' had been housed in a remote camp, set up a little away from the main police unit. Of course, it was without doubt that they provided invaluable information about the whereabouts and the future course of actions of the hardened, core insurgents. But, it also could not be refuted that they used the licence provided to them as the secret hidden arm of the police, exploiting the given authority to settle their own personal scores.

Singh was now armed with invaluable information of the routes they had taken, all those involved in the case, place where they had refueled the vehicle, where they had halted for tea and food etc.

Reinforced with these details, Singh soon managed to twist Avinash's arm enough to make him surrender and accept his mistakes.

But that was not the end. Avinash was a wily fox and not to be outwitted so easily. There still remained a lot of fight in him. "So what is it that you have to say now, after all the facts that have now surfaced in the confessions made by Balvinder, Mohan and the others of your unit," Singh had taken a belligerent stance now.

"Sir, I would not dare to challenge any of the facts revealed in your enquiry. I am convinced that you would not allow any charges to be concocted against me in an attempt to blaspheme my reputation. And, then anyways, a person with your impeccable integrity and professional caliber does not require any further corroboration. Therefore, I have nothing more to say, " Avinash had put up a humble pretence.

"Am I to take it then, that you accept all these charges that you now face", Singh was in no mood to play the cat and mouse game any further. "Well sir, I would rather put up my defence later", clarified Avinash.

"Well, I appreciate that. Law gives the accused the right to remain quiet. So, we will let the prosecution prove its point", chuckled Singh.

"Sir, whatever it is that you may say, it remains a proven fact that but for these 'CAT' operations, there would exist a complete state of anarchy all round, at least, in the present scenario. If you were to delve into the past acts, you could come up with several such incidents where, in the absence of these 'CAT' operations, crime would have reigned supreme, un-checked and unhampered. Take the case of Punjab in the recent past, but for these 'CAT' operations, there was a time when no one dared to pick up cudgels against the rampant militancy. These "CAT operations are common practice amongst the security forces in order to contain militancy and crime. And mind you, they have given very positive results", Avinash supported his case.

"Well, I am not here to go into the mere merits and demerits of the case. As far as I am concerned, there is no legal sanctity to it. The police at best can develop its secret sources and have limited protection as is provided under the 'Evidence Act'. But, we still remain accountable to the law. May be it is an 'in-camera proceedings', Singh responded.

"But Sir, is it not unfair to judge us with a bias? After all, there is no refuting that we've given very positive results. If you have charted down all the follies in the practice, how can you ignore our amazing past records too. My unit, for the past five years or more, has been regarded as the best and the most proactive. In fact, last year our revered Chief had declared my unit as the most outstanding operational battalion," declared Avinash with aplomb.

"Whatever! Gentleman all said and done, the fact remains that in service one is eventually evaluated not for the hundred good performances, but cut to size for the single folly one has committed," came Singh's retort.

"So Sir, according to your esteemed submission, we should not take our tenures here as a challenge to kill insurgency, as a commitment to our motherland to sanctify our land, to cure it of this widespread malignancy, this scourge of militancy. Instead, we should pass the tenure here sitting on our ample butts, sitting on the sidelines allowing the blood bath to continue unaffected. I'm afraid, for any self respecting police official with some balls, that would not be acceptable", Avinash's face had turned a hot red, burning with emotions.

"Hey man! There is no need to get emotional. In all fairness, the law enforcer cannot afford to violate the law himself", Singh remained unaffected by Avinash's burst of emotions.

Avinash was realising that he was not cutting any ice with Singh. So, now he needed to change his tactics. He needed to hit where it would hurt Singh on the personal level. Having realised this, he finally played his master stroke.

"You cannot with your vast years of experience refute a fact, only rogues can deal with rogues. No law abiding citizen ever responds to our requests and urgings for passing on incriminating evidence. The good citizen plays it safe. He wants to stay away from the cross fire. He avoids playing with fire in the fear of burning his fingers. And sir, even you will not refute this fact because in your time as the Commandant you've done the same. We've heard of so many of your exceptional success stories through the CATS fraternity. In fact, you've always been our role model," Avinash had played his final stroke, probably the last in his inventory of departmental tools.

What followed was pin drop silence. Finally, Singh broke the deathly silence.

"Young man, you are playing a dangerous game. Refrain from venturing into this maze till you've mastered this technique. These are dangerous waters. Even if we allow that those ploys give lucrative dividends, how can you justify the multifarous evils that are its by products. The illegal extortions, the smuggling under the garb of the police cover, the immoral killings turning our saviour force into professional killers, for furthering the settling of personal scores of vendetta. Who would you hold responsible for these unscrupulous, inhuman acts of these so called 'CATS' that are your right arm in your mission to eradicate the evils of your society. Don't you realise that you are killing one demon but in the bargain giving birth to innumerable 'demons'. You are so soaked in the glory of your stage managed accomplishments that you have become insensitive to the 'gin' that you have realised to exhume our society. Wake up, man. Your ego is sozzled with the opium of your so called victories and glories. Come out of it and see what you have, in fact, created a dark force that is now rampant and will eventually destroy that what it was created to protect", Singh's words were spouting venom. Avinash stood there, visibly shaken.

"Sir, I believed that I was resorting to a lesser evil to eradicate a greater evil."

Singh's stance softened immediately.

"Avinash, I know for a fact that you are a good soul. Your actions have been a result of your beliefs that were misguided. Your intentions, I realise, were honourable. You had no personal axe to grind. I know for a fact that you are a man of integrity and you did, what you did, was not for personal gains but for the benefit of your people at large. But your actions were misguided, my dear. This is a dangerous game that you have played. You realise of course that if discovered, you would find yourself a very lonely man, with none of your so called sincere colleagues or juniors there, to stand up for your cause. This is an evil world where each man is selfish and cares only for himself and his personal gains!

Do you think this is worth it? Why indulge in such a game, where in the end, only you face the crucification! I learnt this the hard way, my son. So, here I am to advise you, we are not and we cannot be the 'sole contractors' of 'peace'. Eventually, we are only part of this system. Everyone of us is a mere puppet in the game where our strings lie in the hands of the invisible. Hence, stay within the binds, the legal norms limit us. You do the same and let life take its eventual course. Who are we to try and change it", Singh too by now was moved. He had along the way gotten into Avinash's boots. He could feel his predicament too. He gestured to Avinash with his right hand in a show of dismissal. The meeting was over.

Avinash returned to his room, a broken man, no more able to bear the burden of the innumerable medals that now tore at his chest.

* * *

Chapter 13

ITS NOT ABOUT GUNS ALONE

It was a fact we could not ignore!

A major rank officer of the Army along with three soldiers had been killed the previous night in an ambush. The army troops, a strength of eighteen personnel had reportedly surrounded the village number 'four' near Rangia. Eventually, those amongst them that trudged back to their camp were either gravely injured or their weapons and their security vests were wrested away by the insurgents who had attacked their group.

It was still taking some time sinking in. The army could not be defeated, they were the invincible, the perfect force. If they had faced defeat, then this meant the end of everything. If the civil police failed in their effort to control a situation, it was the armed police that came to their rescue and if they also failed to achieve success then the armed forces of the Government, the Army intervened and took control. But what had happened last night just could not be tolerated.

Major General Guru Dayal was a very perturbed man. His authority had been put at stake. He had to get to the bottom of the reasons for this catastrophe. He immediately ordered a high level enquiry in order to unravel the facts.

In the meantime, the intelligence wing of the civil police had managed to collect some inputs. The local police Chief made an effort to pass on this information to the Army top brass. But, he could not cut much ground with them. The Army strictly follow a precedent of conducting their own exclusive enquiries and then pursuing the issue according to their reports that flow from internal fact finding.

The district SP Upendra Morgein was, however, instructed by his peers to go ahead with the necessary investigations.

The Army had also drawn their own deductions. They had decided that the local villagers had a hand to play in this attack on the Army personnel. So, they went ahead and lodged a formal complaint declaring the involvement of the local villagers in the episode.

The villagers too had lodged a cross complaint at this stage, alleging an attack on them by a gang of armed men. They had also specified in their filings that the men, who were involved in this attack on their village, were attired in civilian clothes.

"Sir, the facts are now gradually spilling out. I wonder, have you received the inputs given by the state intelligence unit?" Upendra was speaking to his IG, Mr. Kakoti.

"This and much more. I have a detailed report here with me. Our informer has given certain very interesting tips. The poor unsuspecting Army group was actually lured into a trap. The Major, who has lost his life in the mishap, had very recently developed a source (informer). I wonder if you remember, sometime back we had developed a source whose code number had been "double one", queried Kakoti.

"Oh ya, of course! That emaciated, stunted fellow with deep grey eyes?", quipped Upendra.

"Exactly, he is an old hand at this game. A rogue to the core. He has gradually developed very influential contacts in the administration and even amongst the insurgents. He has inveigled his way into their core. And most interestingly, both the parties are well aware of his shady game, yet they are both using his services for their benefit," informed Kakoti.

"Probably, that's because he has been craftily maneuvering the information he provides so that both parties have benefitted and have got good results to show," analysed Upendra.

"Well, may be. But I believe most of the results are because they have been predetermined and shrewdly arranged by him and his contacts. Anyways, he does give results. However, those amongst who would rather concentrate on the statistical performance levels, without carefully delving deep into the fallouts of their actions, are the ones that eventually fall prey to these dirty game plans of such 'sources'. Probably, the army major was one such prey. And of course, do you remember the Rajeev case", Kakoti explained further.

"Yeah, I'd heard he'd fallen victim to some contrived bait provided by his source", agreed Upendra.

"And my dear, would you have an inkling to who his source was. Yes, it was code "double Nine". That was the reason, why he had been black listed by us and since then we have had nothing to do with him. Rajeev, however, had been livid on realising that he had been taken for a ride. Since then he had been hell bent on liquidating him. And mind you, he had been hot on his trail but the bastard managed to save his hide by involving a local MLA. The MLA raised some embarrassing issues in the assembly forcing Rajeev to withdraw.

Since then "double Nine" too has stayed away from the police, fearing for his life. But, as I have learnt, 'double-one' has now been operating for 'double-nine'.

Unfortunately for the major who got taken in by him, as for sometime he had been working for the major, and this was the end result of the major's interaction with this wily creature", sympathised Kakoti.

"This is really serious. Somebody needs to stand up and watch out for him there. Else some other unsuspecting army soldiers will continue to be targeted by his kind."

"Anyways, I have done some searchings, and the information that I have come up with, is that a few days ago an army recruit, Prajapat, had molested a girl of that village. The villagers had then approached the Major as Prajapat belonged to his unit with their complaint. The Major, however, had refused to entertain their complaint and had in fact bad mouthed them. The villagers had then left in a huff, visibly very disturbed", informed Upendra.

"That's good going! So, this confirms my source's information too. By the way, how exactly did you come by this piece of information?", interjected Kakoti.

"Actually sir, after the Major refused to lend them his ear, the villagers had approached me. I had then got a formal complaint registered. Since then we have been following it up with careful investigation.

Then some of these villagers who have joined our 'Village Defence Force' team had later confirmed that a group of insurgents led by Gohein, on hearing of this incident, had approached the villagers. Smart cookies that they are, they had smelled the possibility of encashing on the situation. So they had acted immediately. They visited the simple villagers, inciting them with their false show of sympathy. They assured them that they were aggrieved too at such blasé exploitation by the forces of these peace loving people. They promised them that they could not be mere bystanders and watch their brethrens treated so shabbily. They gradually convinced the villagers that they would help them to get their revenge. And that is how the insurgents and villagers joined hands", elaborated Upendra.

"But, I thought you said that you had an active 'Village Defence Force' group working for you. Why did they not bring you this information before hand?" questioned a puzzled Kakoti.

"Their explanation to us was that they had no inkling of such an immediate reprisal being on the cards. They said that they had intended to inform us during our next weekly meeting which had been due after two days hence", spoke Upendra.

"I think its time for some action on our part. We have the right leads, lets act upon it. Collect the beaten constables of that village, and also instruct the special investigation squad to get on the job. We now need to get to the minute details of how exactly they conducted it", instructed an excited Kakoti.

"But sir, we have a problem. The Army is averse to our further intrusions on the matter".

"I know! They now want to put the whole affair under wraps as they fear that when it surfaces it shall expose them in a very poor light. Poor things, their stature is at stake! They would rather declare it as just an unfortunate operational failure on the part of their slain officer, the Major.

"Nevertheless, you are hereby formally instructed by me to carry on with the investigations. When I have given you the instructions whats keeping you? We cannot let the likes of Gohein and that son of a ......get away with it. They are getting too big for their boots! They now need a taste of their own medicine. How dare they encroach on my territory. We need to teach them a lesson they shall not easily forget. So, its decided. Go ahead with my instructions. In the meantime I need to move now. There is a meeting scheduled with the Chief Secretary in connection with this case only", Kakoti got up to leave.

Kakoti was not only well experienced but also a very smart cop. He had already analysed the pros and cons involved, so he had a prior briefing session with both his DGP as well as the Chief Secretary and smoothly managed to put into their ears the details of the course of action decided with Upendra. Some revenue authorities too had already imparted some of the details to the Chief Secretary. The meeting went ahead as scheduled in the Secretariate. The Chief Secretary asked the Major General Guru Dayal to put forth his point of view first.

"May I inform you that our internal enquiry has been thoroughly undertaken and completed. We have found that there have been some operational lapses on the part of our troops. However, four of the major defaulters have already paid the price with their lives. We have already issued proceedings against the remaining. Hence, as far as we are concerned, the matter has been efficiently dealt with and the chapter now stands closed", announced the Major General.

Nobody seated there was a fool. They were all old hands at this game. The message had gone loud and clear.

Yet, the Chief Secretary lifted an eyebrow making eye contact with the DGP who, in turn, gently changed his posture to wink at Kakoti.

Taking the clue, immediately Kakoti intervened, "Sir, I'm afraid there are still several loose ropes to be tackled. Nine weapons and six bullet proof jackets are yet to be recovered", but before he could complete what he had to say, he was interrupted by the Major General, "That's our headache. We shall deal with it. I have already drawn up a plan to surround the village and conduct a thorough search. We have reliable information that they are still with the villagers who were involved in the incident".

"For all we know, you may be right. But do you realise that by doing so you would be exposing the army to a greater threat, a grave retaliation which may result in things getting totally out of hand. If you should march in that area, you could be in more trouble than you can handle. Have you been reading the local newspapers lately? Have you then read the articles already tarnishing the Army's image? As it is, it has taken a serious beating recently. Would you like to face more flak from the common man? The local politicians have been having a field day at your expense. They have been demanding the withdrawal of the army from these areas under the pretext that the army is now no more our protector. Rather, they are pitting you with nefarious intentions. The proof of it, they say, is in the fact that these troops are moving around in civvies. Why? they ask. Where was the need to hide in civilian garb? So sir, if you were to ask me, for the present you should stay away from the scene of action and let us help you instead", justified a crafty Kakoti, thrilled to see the General's discomfiture. Pricked by this, Guru Dayal thundered, "What possible other intentions could we have? Even the thought is preposterous! How dare they!"

"Sir, that is exactly how we feel too. But you know the masses. Once their tongues are set wagging, it's difficult to be heard for sometime. Like the Chinese whisper, the tale has spread. It shall take sometime for the common man to see sense now. So sir, why play with fire then?" Kakoti had made his point.

The Chief Secretary realised it was time for him to intervene, "Don't misunderstand us. We are only worried for you and want that the weapons should be recovered and public perception fairly managed."

"And for that, we need your cooperation. We must first lodge a clear cut FIR without holding back any facts and figures. We shall do our best to support you.

We assure you the arms shall be recovered and handed over. I feel it is my moral duty to update you further. We have managed to get hold of a mediator who would help", added the DGP.

"Oh by the way, will the local MLA Haroon cooperate? He carries a lot of clout here, I've heard", enquired the Chief Secretary.

"Well sir, he really has no other option left", grinned a snug DGP, "everything can not be settled with guns!"

Picking up the clue from his boss, Kakoti informed the Major General, "Sir if you wish, it may help to sit down together separately. We can then decide the further course of action. If you should agree, we can meet at Rangia Police Station today late evening. You could send over a responsible team....", Kakoti let his sentence float in the air incomplete.

All heads nodded in agreement – the present meeting was annulled with the Chief Secretary's parting shot that he wanted immediate action to be taken on the matter and its report submitted in his office within the next two days.

The very next morning, the villagers had a visitor, the local MLA. Very soon after, the village defence force members transported all the missing guns and security vests of the army personnel to the local Police station. Thus, they all came to be accounted for, though, they were returned in a pathetic condition, as they had all been ripped apart by the frustrated villagers. Obviously, the helpless lot had no option but to vent their rage on them.

Thereafter, a long telephonic exchange between Kakoti and Haroon followed.

Haroon delivered all the details, confirming the annoyance over the molestation, and that after the refusal by the authorities to take any action against the culprit, the villagers had responded to Gohein's suggestions whereupon the gory killings had happened.

Gohein had intervened and, taking advantage of the vulnerable state of mind of the villagers, had arranged the attack on the army troops with the support of Shubroto, in fact, known by the code 'double one'.

Shubroto had, thereafter, prompted Major Subhash to lead the troops in civilian clothings, reasoning with the Major that it would ensure their easy and unnoticed entry into the village. Shubroto, however, was only the prompter, the king pin behind this dirty game had been Gohein. The troops fell into their trap. They were far outnumbered and the outcome was that Major Subhash and three of his men were shot down on the spot. The others suffered serious injuries, too.

They did not stand a chance against the carefully masterminded planned attack on them by the insurgents, with the support of the aggrieved villagers.

Of course, the villagers insisted that they had attacked the army personnel mistaking them for dacoits who were moving in plain clothings. Army never moved without their uniform, did they? The excuse appeared perfectly plausible, though foolhardy!

Anyways, Kakoti promised Haroon that the cases against the villagers after initial arrest would be dropped provided Gohein and Shubroto were handed over to the police. Haroon gave his assurance that he would do the needful and, in due course, vital information about their locations would be provided.

The concerned police officials and army personnel delivered their complete reports to their seniors.

Lessons had been picked up and carefully learnt.

A hurried meeting was called. This time, everybody maintained a studied silence. Threadbare facts were taken up. Arguments and disagreements were carefully avoided. Corrective measures were assured. With the recovery of the weapons, some material was now available to show that the administration had taken due steps. Some arrests were also declared. Everybody was now satisfied. However, the main perpetrators were still roaming free and had not fallen in the police dragnet as yet.

Kakoti had the last word. Addressing the other Chiefs of the armed forces, his was a gloating tone as he pompously advised, "Sir, in the future, kindly ensure that your troops also take along a few representatives of the local police whenever they should plan any such coups!"

★ ★ ★

Chapter 14

ALL PART OF THE GAME

It was their day of celebrations in the sixteenth battalion of the Central Armed Police. Commandant Sunil Kumar was personally extolling the achievements of his unit. And why not! A team of his unit led by his young, strapping and dynamic Deputy Commandant, Sanjeev, had had an enthralling encounter with a group of insurgents. The praiseworthy feature of the encounter had been that they had managed to shoot down three insurgents, including one core commander and a divisional head, without any loss at all to their own force. In addition, they had recovered a huge consignment of arms, ammunitions and explosives too.

"Hats off to you! Its an amazing feat! A fantastic job! You deserve the gallantry medal. You have made us truly proud," Sunil Kumar applauded the team.

"Sir, if it were not for your able and constant guidance…'" Sanjeev modestly made an attempt to pass on the credit to the Battalion Chief.

"Aw! come on, shed the modesty. You are the hero! A special dinner to celebrate the occasion is now on the cards tonight. Let the wine flow. Drink away, get sozzled, you deserve the fun, enjoy it man. Go have a blast tonight!", Sunil made a grandiose announcement and left the assembly hall.

Sanjeev followed his boss enroute to the Officers' Mess. Sunil continued, obviously wanting to know more from the man on the scene where the action had taken place, "Download the details. I am truly excited at the outcome."

"Sir, I wonder if you recall a slimy looking character, bald headed with bowed shoulders and a slight drag in his stride. If you remember you had taken an instinctive dislike to this man. But, he was a resourceful guy with the right contacts and an approach in the core group of the insurgents. So, very reluctantly you had agreed and we had inducted him as one of our sources (secret informers).

"Oh of course! How can I forget that same rascal who had demanded twenty thousand bucks and a bottle of Vodka from you", reflected Sunil.

"Exactly sir, you've truly got a sharp memory. He had made an ass out of me and I was truly peeved. So I had been raring for his blood for a long time", added Sanjeev.

"Oh really! This comes as news to me. You never let this out on me. You are a sly one, aren't you. I would have accompanied you hence", chided Sunil.

"Sir, I'm really sorry. But I had no inkling of how reliable his inputs were. On three occasions in the past, nothing had come out of his intelligence feeds. But, this time things fitted into the desired slots and they just clicked. In fact, I had pondered on it for sometime, unsure whether it made sense to follow up the information provided by him. On three earlier occasions we had fully geared up for the operations but it had turned out to be a damp squib. So I was in two minds whether it would be worthwhile following it up or not.

In fact, we eventually did leave for the operation but very half-heartedly. Thank God for the gut feeling at the last minute, which made me include our quick reaction team too with us.

I must give them the major credit for tackling the situation so well. If it had not been for their quick witted close cooperation and well synchronised reactions, we may have had an altogether different tale to tell.

Sir, it was about two o'clock in the afternoon. It was a particularly sultry and humid day when that fellow 'Baldy', I had nicknamed him 'Tatoo', gave me a call. We talked for almost half an hour. Thereafter, I immediately called the QRT of our unit and instructed them to get on the double and verify the places mentioned by Tatoo. Enquiries indicated that his words carried weight this time, so we decided to launch the operation. I made it a point to take Tatoo along with me with a clear warning that if this time things should go wrong, I would shoot him on the spot. I had had enough of this cat and mouse game that he had been playing with us so far.

On reaching the instructed spot, we laid the ambush and waited. We had reached the spot on foot from different directions, carefully following the drill in order to avoid any landmines enroute. We waited patiently. Three hours went past. The sun had set. Visibility had gone down considerably when we noticed a few men, they appeared to be armed, slowly approaching the spot. Initially, our reaction was a little uncertain. We were worried if once again Tatoo was up to his usual tricks and was two timing us. But 'Tatoo' kept reassuring us that he had no intentions of crossing over.

Time seemed to have come to a standstill when the group moved in, almost imperceptibly. We waited with bated breath, and then as soon as the group moved in, within our firing range, I gave the signal and we had them covered from all sides. We opened fire; they retaliated immediately firing in the direction of our fire. But this time we had a distinct advantage. The crossfire continued for almost twenty odd minutes. Then, it appears we got lucky. Our bullets found the targets that mattered, we had hit their leaders. As soon as they lost the core leaders, the rest fled leaving behind their weaponry in their desperation to escape the line of fire. Probably the leaders were ahead of the group and came in the line of our fire first. Tatoo pointed them out to us. The local police SHO too arrived on the scene and confirmed the same."

"Okay", interjected Sunil, "So where is our hero Tatoo now! He deserves the medals, what do you say?" chuckled Sunil.

"Sir, we have duly rewarded him for his feat."

"And what's that"?

"Well, I have sent him packing to his permanent abode. He deserved it and we have obliged", informed Sanjeev.

"You mean, you have knocked him off?"

"Exactly sir, he was an unreliable bastard! He could not be trusted any further. I decided that we could not take any more chances with him. Sir, I am sorry, but I made this decision without consulting you. It needed to be taken, right then and there, Sir. We disposed off his body which was recovered later on by the SHO in some other case. The chap had a terrible criminal history and was in the 'wanted' list anyways", added Sanjeev.

They had in the meantime reached the mess where the others were already waiting to join in the celebrations.

It was already eleven at night. But today, nobody was in a hurry to eat and turn in for the day. It was the night of celebrations. Drinks flowed, men sweated it out on the dance floors till their feet refused to carry them any further, loud music blared across the hall. The dinner hours stretched on and on with loads of compliments coming Sanjeev's way.

Then the days slipped by. However, the intelligence reports kept pouring in at odd intervals that there were the possible chances of an attack on their unit. The insurgents were obviously baying for revenge. The entire unit members were given very strict instructions to follow due precautions, particularly against the possible use of explosives by the insurgents. News had been filtering in that they had now in their possession new improvised devices that could be lethal. But nothing happened. Minutes turned into hours, hours into days, days into weeks and then into months without any untoward incident taking place.

Laxity crept in gradually.

"They would not have the balls to come within a mile of our purview, far less dare to touch us", came a pompous declaration by the sub inspector to the company Havaldar.

"Sir, very frankly. I can't fathom why our officers are reacting the way they have been. These 'day in day out reminders' to be alert, these precautions are almost on the verge of being ridiculous. How long can we move around like this?" reacted the Havaldar.

"It is a fact that it is next to impossible to expect us to check each hole on these roads for possible IED implants. After all, look at these roads, they are truly an excuse for a road, with so many pot holes! But anyways, we have been asked to take these steps for our own welfare and safety. Hence, we really must conduct all these safety drills", instructed the cautious sub-inspector.

"Sir, may be then we should add the sniffer dogs to accompany us. They are said to be really good at smelling out these hidden explosives", added Havaldar.

"I have been told that the seniors are already considering that", declared the sub-inspector, as he walked away ending the discussion.

Another week went by. Sanjeev received the latest update that the insurgents had killed a couple of villagers in Khori village and snatched some rations and other provisions.

Sanjeev rationalised this to mean that insurgents had probably antagonised the Khori dwellers. The villagers should obviously be angry with the insurgents. Sanjeev felt that the villagers could be responsive to the police queries and pass on information regarding the insurgents willingly. So, Sanjeev left for Khori immediately along with his team members.

As he approached the village, on a blind turn, there were a series of blasts in quick succession followed by a volley of shots fired from an overlooking hillock.

Sanjeev fell unconscious. He had been hit and was bleeding profusely. When he regained his consciousness, he could see only blood splattered all around. He recognised a few of his men, some of them lay there disfigured, their limbs blown away, their remains sprawled in an awkward inhuman like posture. He recognised the remains of his Havaldar's uniform; his human form had been disfigured beyond recognition, bits and pieces of yanked away guts lay splattered all over. Sanjeev's vision blurred, the blood oozing down his forehead had begun to matt just above his lashes. He could see no living member of his party as far as he could decipher. He could feel the weakness coming upon him due to the excessive loss of blood. He was once again beginning to lose consciousness. Somehow, he managed to pass a message through his wireless to his unit – 'They had been ambushed, there had been a very heavy loss of life. Chances of any member surviving the attack were very bleak'. He could hear the gun shots coming closer, obviously the attackers were closing in on them, probably shooting down at close range those remaining wounded soldiers who were still alive. He could faintly discern the abuses they were showering on them. He could hear their jeers and the insane cries of jubiliation, the screeches, the delirious shouts as he began to slowly lose consciousness again. Sanjeev's initial reactions had been to retaliate, to kill them all, but he realised he could not. He knew he was going to die. Faces of his two little boys, both twins, swam across his vision and then faded away. As he made one last-ditch effort to move, a bullet pierced his head, leaving an ugly gaping wound. He let off one last deep sigh and then was lost to the world forever.

As soon as Sunil received the frantic message from his ambushed men, he left for their assistance. But the going for him was not easy. He had sufficient experience behind him to realise that the insurgents, expecting follow up troops, would have laid out blast landmines and would be waiting to ambush them enroute. Hence, Sunil was forced to break up his party into three different segments and they had to undertake different routes through unfriendly difficult forests, abandoning the normal faster paths. So, over three hours had lapsed before he finally arrived at the scene. The sight that awaited him was blood-curdling. A chill ran down his spine. Ripped fragments of human limbs lay strewn all over. The entire area presented a ghastly picture. Obviously, the explosives used had been very potent and had left behind lethal consequences. He instructed his men to search carefully through the horrifying mess in order to come up with some pieces of evidence. They finally came up with strips of wire. It looked like they had used an IED that had been set off using command wires. Insurgents evidently had ample spare hours to search through the victims' personal belongings. They had walked away with all the police arms and ammunitions too. There remained not a single survivor amongst the whole party led by Sanjeev. Sunil just stood there stunned too shaken to react. Slowly, emotions surfaced and tears ran down his cheeks. The fellow soldiers stood there unable to bear their shame as they realised how they had failed to save their friends. They had met with a brutal end. Slowly, Sunil controlled himself and in a clipped tone ordered his troops to clean up the mess. A few of them were put on area domination and sentry duties, others were ordered to carefully collect all the remains. In the meanwhile, the area DIG, on hearing of this terrible mishap, had informed Sunil that he was on his way to the site.

Sunil ordered the officers back at the unit to arrange for the coffins and to inform all the relatives concerned on the local addresses of the deceased soldiers and his officers. A guard of honour was to be arranged. Coffins were to be mobilised to carry the dead.

Nobody looks forward to such chores. But then, they were alive while their friends were dead. Though disliking it, there was no shirking from the responsibility. And so they marched back with the remains of seventeen soldiers and two officers to their unit. A sinking feeling of despair was gradually overtaking them. The battalion headquarters bore the look of a graveyard. Their meals in the mess remained untouched. There was not one amongst them who felt hungry that day.

After a short lapse of time, the DIG, Shri Mahendra also returned to the headquarters, having visited the site. Then the formalities of the Guard of Honour were conducted and the bodies dispatched to their respective destinations. After all, the documentation formalities were completed. Later in the evening, the DIG along with the Commandant made a visit to the barracks and spoke individually to all the jawans in an effort to boost their deflated morale.

All said and done, though the troops were temporarily downcast, yet on the other hand, there was now ignited in their hearts, the intense desire to take revenge. They all wanted to hit out at the insurgents. They wanted their friends' avenged. Not one amongst them felt otherwise.

So now the battle was on.

The very next day Mahendra held a 'sammellan'. He enquired at large if the jawans would like to be moved to some other location and get replaced by fresh troops? There rose from the crowd a loud cry of resistance. The crowd howled back visibly annoyed at the insinuation - "Are we cowards? We shall stay back. This is all about guerilla warfare. All part of the game. Now we want you to give us the signal to track down each one of these killers. We want revenge. And we shall not rest till we have it", screamed the affronted crowd.

Relieved, Mahendra, showered the crowd with fitting compliments, assuaged their hurt egos and then left. New officers and men soon came in to fill in the vacuum left by the unfortunate departed souls.

Future events bear testimony to the glorious fact that this Battalion performed heroically in every scenario. They contained the local insurgency. Sunil recalled the next Republic Day that was celebrated. Eight Gallantry Medals were announced for his men. They were all posthumous gallantry medals awarded to his late friends, Sanjeev and his teammates. They were awarded to them for having wiped out four of the core leaders of the insurgents. It was different that very soon after this amazing feat of theirs, they had lost their lives in a counter ambush.

But then, that is all a part of this game.

* * *

Chapter 15

SPECIAL OPERATIONS

Special operations or crime drives have now become the order of the day. Particularly, in those areas where the essential social institutions have collapsed owing to multiple pressures and distortions. Our fast declining values today have expedited the degeneration, as they have become the last straw that breaks the camel's back.

Special drives have now become the accepted way of life in most of the government functioning.

And, whenever public outcry crosses all proportions, thanks to the stifling ghettos of misadministration and blatant red tapism, then one is forced to resort to what is referred to as the 'special drive'. These drives, however, are successful in providing only temporary relief for very short durations.

We all are well aware of various such drives, for instance, the sterilization drives, literacy drives and the anti poverty drives. In these cases some progress actually takes place, while some is projected statistically and the remaining lost in mere intellectual discussions.

Then, may be in personal life too, we are adopting a similar style of working out our lives particularly when they involve areas of our health and our religion.

Whatever may be the impact of these special drives on public life but when it relates to the complex arenas of people's life and death then it assumes great criticality. And the police, in particular, presents an abhorring picture involving these spheres.

Prateek, had just completed around ten years of his service. He had in this period been exposed to a lot that had taken him by surprise. He had completed his post graduation before taking the civil services examination. On succeeding, he had started off his career on a sincere note, though in all honesty joining the police force had really not been his aspiration. However, as a self actualised, self respecting human being, he had made up his mind to put in his very best into his job.

Initially, still trying to get hold of the strings and fathom the nature of his job requirements, he kept flowing along with his departmental tide. Consequently, he felt destabilised for sometime. However, gradually the realisation started to dawn upon him that he would need to swim against the tide, if he wanted his own peace of mind. But, by the time he had gathered enough courage and conviction to do so, much water had already flown under the bridge.

However, its never really late to make a fresh start in one's life. And, one particular incident in Prateek's professional life really rattled his conscience. He felt so small, so belittled. He felt he was the biggest sinner breathing in this big, wide evil world. His lips were sealed. He felt helpless, inadequate to speak, he felt he had no face left to show, in fact.

And even today, when he recalls the episode, it bothers him deeply and leaves him considerably restless. But he still has not been able to gather together the gumption to acknowledge the dark truth. Not that he alone finds himself in such a predicament. There are scores of them here and some are even adorned with decorations, medals and the works which they proudly carry on their loathsome shoulders.

The incident relates to the time when Prateek had barely completed five years of his tenure in service. Usually, sufficient evidence is never made available against the insurgents, mostly owing to the fear factor that their presence generates in the common man. Hence, it was a case of an implied drill in his department to wipe off the target groups in an encounter and not much focus was laid upon their possible arrests. In all fairness, in all the official review meetings too, it is always the daunting figures of their killings that draw general applause and commendation. It cannot be denied that silent communications can convey a lot more and it is these that put the seal of truth on the unaccounted for and uncontrolled distortions. Anyways, this happened to be Prateek's first independent charge. He had just received the message that troops across the Brahmaputra barrage were engaged in an encounter and that the firing was still going on.

Prateek left immediately for the place of the incident and joined his force in the action. It was very soon reported to him that one of the insurgents had been shot and his weapons recovered while the rest had fled, taking advantage of the cover of darkness. Prateek then took a detailed briefing from his Deputy Superintendent along with the other officers and then proceeded to return to the headquarters, where an eager press entourage awaited him. The press enthused about the police achievement in all the papers the next day.

But soon followed a complaint against the encounter and that was forwarded to Prateek. The Station House Officer (SHO) was then summoned to comment on the same, "Sir, please do not pay heed to this scrap of paper. The locals here are absolute rascals. This is a living example of politicking for compensation. And that is all that there is to it", the SHO had explained it away to the ignorant SP.

"Okay!", was Prateek's initial reaction.

"Sir, why bother, anyways the magisterial enquiry is already on. Within no time everything would become crystal clear for all to see", the SHO advised.

Prateek dismissed him and then earmarked the complaint to the Dy. SP of the area. The magisterial enquiry came to a quick resolve. Three of the officers involved in the incident were decorated with medals.

But luck had something else planned out for Prateek. Destiny plays complex games. So very soon after, destiny led Prateek to the village and the house of the slain insurgent. Prateek was flicking through the village crime note book in the local chowki when his eyes fell on the name 'Sapan', something clicked within him. Was it not the name of the insurgent who had recently been liquidated in the Brahmaputra barrage encounter.

Something seemed to not quite fit here. He immediately ordered a meeting with the local villagers. During the course of listening to their complaints an old, frail woman with her back bent over with age, slowly stood up within the midst and sought an exclusive interview with the 'S.P. Sahib'. She said she had been made a victim in the dirty games played by the bigwigs. She admonished the system and announced for all to listen that if the S.P. was truly interested in resolving their woes, then he should follow her to her house which was only at a distance of 600 yards from where they were positioned.

It was a small, very basic construction consisting of only a single room. The household items were few but neatly arranged. On an initial overview one could gaze that the house belonged to cultured people. Overlooking the main door was a photo hanging on the wall with a wreath of dry flowers adorning it. The face looked familiar but Prateek failed to recollect who it had belonged to.

"Sahib, this is my son. Those two little children playing on the cot are my grandchildren and this is my daughter-in-law", introduced the old lady.

"I am sorry to learn that now your son is no more, but how did he happen to die! Was he seriously sick?", Prateek sympathised.

"No, my son was a perfectly hale and hearty young strapping youth. But he became the unfortunate victim of the social miasmas that inflict our society."

"Sorry! I am afraid you have me lost, state the reasons clearly, amma", Prateek wanted a clarification.

"My son was born here to me in this very village. We had somehow managed and sent him to the city to be educated. So he returned a well educated and an outspoken young lad who spoke on behalf of the ignorant villagers against the injustice being meted out to them. In the bargain he earned the wrath of some of the influential people of this area. Initially, they tried to break his spirit through verbal threats, but my son was a self respecting youth. He refused to be cowed down. So, they finally got him involved in some fake cases. In collaboration with your local police authorities these cases were registered against him and ...." She broke down, tears rolled down her dry emaciated cheeks.

"Are you telling me that the police registered false cases against your son? Mai do you realise the gravity of your insinuations?"

"What is the purpose of my accusations now. They shall not bring back my son. I had warned him repeatedly to keep to himself. I told him he would not achieve anything by playing the role of the local samaritan. I kept telling him to stop, it would do him no good instigating the local 'dadas'. But all my entreaties fell on deaf ears, he refused to budge from his stance. I'd even advised him to go and lie supine before the lords and beg for forgiveness. I had myself gone begging them to overlook the lapse on my son's part. But the damage was done. They had vowed vendetta against my poor hapless son. All those that he had fought for, conveniently turned away and looked the other way. Why would anybody stretch their necks out for him. They were not fools like him. I don't really know how, but the 'Dadas' hand in glove with your police, somehow projected my poor son as an open ground worker for the insurgents", her voice cracked and gradually crumbled. The room resonated with the release of the bottled up grief that had been eating away into this family. They all cried unashamed.

The pain in their sobs had shaken Prateek, "Then.....?" he persisted.

"They took him away. We were left with no source of income and four mouths to feed. Somehow we scrounged and managed to muster just about enough to survive. He had been jailed for six months. Then he was released on bail. He returned, a mere shadow of his earlier self, a man who had been so full of beans and energy now seemed to be left without a soul. He came back to us, a mute member of our family with nothing to say, nothing to declare. Though he had never complained to us. Yet I was his mother, I could read the pain, the humiliation that he had obviously undergone in this period. He returned and quietly took to farming the small plot of land that our family owned. But only a few days had lapsed, when a man came to our house and took him away on some false pretext.

He did not return home that night. We spent the whole night anxiously counting the hours as they lumbered past. Morning arrived with the news that 'Sapan', my son, had been killed. They had bumped him off in an encounter enlisting him under the category of the insurgents."

As she pronounced the name, lightning struck. It was a bolt out of the blue that had hit Prateek. He stood up with a jerk. The name with the face of the man in the picture frame hanging on her wall flashed past. A series of happenings did a quick replay in his mind. His heart beat rose thudding at a threatening pace. The old woman pleaded, "Sahib, he was the sole support who had to see me through my old age. Look at this girl here, she has been widowed at an age when girls are still carefree. And here, she is saddled with these two little brats and a whole life to contend with. These little ones probably have no or very indistinct memories left with them of their father. What was their mistake? How were we to blame that we have been left behind in this predicament? Sir, you are a 'barra' police officer. We know you cannot get us back our Sapan but you can punish his killers. If you are a man with any self respect, promise this old hag that you will revenge my son. I want the heads of those killer cops who have killed my innocent son. Promise me sahib, you will do this for me. Only then will I be able to die in peace. May God bless you!", came the cry from the mother raring for revenge and then suddenly her entire frail form curled into a twisted posture and shook with heart wrenching sobs.

The daughter-in-law who had all this while stood in the corner silently sobbing moved closer to her mother-in-law in an effort to consol her. Passing Prateek, she directed a deep reproachful look. Looking then deep into his eyes she hissed, "Congratulations, sahib, for the medal", and then accusing tears rolled down her cheeks. Her mute resistance had registered.

Prateek suddenly felt so small, so insignificant in front of the widow. He stood there fully exposed, naked in her full view. He could feel the floor beneath his feet beginning to cave in. He was her thief and had been caught red handed.

Slowly he gathered himself together and walking up to the old woman, barely patting her assured, "I know amma, I know the whole case, I shall do what best I can!"

Prateek returned. The day's happenings had left him a shattered man. All the way back to the camp the thought kept troubling him, "How many innocents were sacrificed every year. Used as baits to satiate the hunger pangs of those with muscle. Do we have the right to commit such sacrilege? There we have questions being raised on whether we have the right to carry out capital punishment even in cases where the guilt has been proved. And here we are sacrificing innocent lives to further our individual cause. Does society have the right to kill its members if it has failed to take proper care, to provide them with an environment which is conducive to their proper growth and development?"

Really, to work unaffected in such circumstances is difficult for a person with emotions that are still alive within him and keep bothering him. Of course, there are others that will commit much more heinous acts without batting an eyelid and they are very successful people too!

Prateek had reached home. He called for his SHO in his camp office. The SHO arrived immediately hearing that the matter was of importance. He stood at attention waiting for instructions.

"Why did you do it? Deceived us! why?", Prateek's voice announced a helplessness in his subdued tone.

"I don't understand sir", reacted the bemused SHO.

"Sapan, he was no 'open ground worker', he was innocent. He had nothing at all to do with insurgents. Then why? Where was your conscience when you guys took him away from his home, stage managed an encounter and worst of all, you forwarded a misleading message to me as well? You involved me in this heinous act of yours?", Prateek was slowly losing control. He was livid now, his frustration was now finding a release.

"Sir, you have been wrongly informed. The man had a long criminal history. He was by no means innocent, sir. And it is an unwritten precedent to pick up such trouble makers and bump them off, sir. Otherwise they go scot free and openly flout the law. It is just not possible to get them otherwise. And for that matter even the magisterial enquiry did not find any foul play in the proceedings. Janab himself has been decorated with a medal in that case", SHO completed his carefully calculated explanation.

Prateek felt stupid. He found himself at a loss of words for a while. Who was to blame? Probably, he himself too! How many of the encounters conducted by our police force are for real? Probably not even a meager nine to ten percent. Prateek realised he was helpless. He alone could not fight the system. If he tried, he would be wiped out. He was fast realising he dared not muster enough courage to spell out the truth. However, he needed to cleanse some of the blood that had soiled his hands. He needed to attempt to absolve his soul somewhat, so he finally decided that he would extend whatever financial aid he could to Sapan's family, to rid his conscience of at least some of the burden that it carried.

Many years have rolled past since this incident took place. But nothing has really changed, nothing really ever changes. Still, bodies are exhumed. Enquires are lost forever under the monumental heap of files. When things get out of hand, then some vouch for reforms and then the reports of these reform commissions are stowed away to gather dust.

So, even these reforms are now mere drives that have a short life span probably a couple of months and then die out a quick natural death.

We are living in a 'pseudo – world' of 'special operations'. Hail! The Keepers of Peace! The subverters have all fled the scene!

* * *

Chapter 16

CHARRED BAMBOOS

This tale is set in a region that has not witnessed any progress for years. The area does not have any metalled roads, not even the basic infrastructure to account for. People survive at the mercy of nature and the rain gods.

And to add to their woes and these vagaries of nature, the local people also have to bear human atrocities. Their lot would force even a true democrat to hang his head in shame. It was almost as if all the signs of modernisation avoided the region like the 'pariah'.

There was little or no education amongst them, they lived a life of abject penury and deprivation, superstitious beliefs controlled their lives, outdated traditions and inhuman practices still dominated their existence.

"Ah! It seems finally some commission has bothered to visit us from Delhi to conduct enquiries into the plight of the dwellers here. The cops have been seen moving their butts, scurrying to and fro, all dressed in ceremonial finery", the self proclaimed social worker derided the system.

"Why, what made this happen?", came a casual curious response from his local friend as he crushed some tobacco leaves between his palms.

"People are talking that half a dozen tribal women have been raped. Their modesty outraged, you know".

"That's a fine piece of wit to begin the day. Raped, why would anybody in his senses want to rape them? They are anyways freely available for a pittance. That's ludicrous reasoning".

Their gossip session was brought to an abrupt end as two-three police jeeps zipped past raising a tremendous cloud of dust all round them, forcing the two to shut their mouth tight and cover their faces with both their hands.

After the dust had settled somewhat, the two got up, deciding to follow the jeeps to the police chowki and find out what the commotion was all about.

In the police chowki, Mrs. Manorama, the head of an NGO 'ASHA' was involved in an intriguing discussion with some of the members of the commission that had landed here to enquire into some matters.

Manorama had been trying for years to uplift the state of the tribal women here. She had been working against the gross exploitation of these women. She had been striving hard for the past ten years in a selfless, totally committed way. Today she had turned 55. She had, over the years, won implicit faith and deep respect amongst the locals there, for the selfless quality of her dedication to the cause of this deprived and exploited community. A simple lifestyle, with the very bare minimum needs for survival, a straightforward mind set, a commitment that was truly praiseworthy, an attire that exemplified simplicity, were her trademarks. She had spent the last ten years in a pair of 'white' saris with a thin green border and a pair of rubber slippers which had outlived their utility and were still, though not very successfully, attempting to protect her feet from the heat and the grime of the roads they traversed.

So far, Manorama had not been too verbose before the members of the commission. She had avoided revealing candid facts probably because she was trying to gauge the sincerity of the team members, in particular, their Chairman Mr. Ram Kumar.

Manorama had had the bitter experience of seeing several such commissions come and go in these last ten years. They would come, but very often the red tape would prevent access to these people. Even if some offered an open access to them, they finally came across not as people who were really interested in the upliftment of the locals but as someone who were merely some media hype and the like. She was still dilly-dallying, wondering whether enlightening this lot would bring any concrete response. In the last ten years she had knocked at innumerable doors begging for help. So much so, that now she had lost track of how many.

However, her gut feeling was urging her to believe that this man, Mr. Ram Kumar was made of different stuff, he meant business. She made up her mind. She would unload before him all that she knew or had experienced.

She began, "Sir, if I may.... as long as the Government goes on casually sidelining the dire need for investing in the development of the infrastructure of this area, unless they encourage the establishment of fresh educational institutions that offer an opportunity to the locals to have basic education and enlightenment, such incidents will keep reoccurring and no one will react or take some concrete steps to prevent them".

"Okay, and so....." Ramkumar was showing a growing interest in the lady's declaration.

"Would you believe that this area is totally bereft of any source of proper employment and income? Even agriculture is so basic that you cannot put together two square meals a day. Obviously, people are so poor that...."

"How do they manage then....?"

"Oh, they toil in the forest. The contractors there employ these poor souls for a mere ten rupees a day wage. Unfortunately for them they get employment here only for about 3-4 months in the whole year."

"Oh God! Do you mean to say that the per capita income is much below the poverty level here," Ramkumar spoke in the typical urban dialect.

Manorma reacted, "Its funny you should use the term 'income' for these people here. Most families out here are surviving solely on five kilograms of grain in a month. They grind the grain into fine powder and then add two to three spoonfuls of it into plain water and just gulp it down for one square meal a day".

No wonder the locals here are both physically as well as mentally unfit.

"Women put up their skeletal frames with little or no meat on them for sale. You will probably find it difficult to believe but women here are up for sale for a paltry sum of five rupees. Yet, there are cases where women are brutally molested, raped, tortured but nobody gives them a penny for their sufferings. This land has stopped reacting to such happenings. There are bigger issues that they need to deal with, survival is one, food to fill their tummies another. And even if aware, they will not divulge."

"That's really strange. Would you believe that the newspapers in Delhi are screaming headlines of this episode and the matter has been taken up even in the parliament", reflected a perplexed Ram Kumar.

"I am well aware of that, yesterday, the district collector, along with the Superintendent of Police, had visited the area too. They came and had some statements recorded. Orders were given and a few women underwent medical examinations. The reports that were produced indicated that the women in question were used to regular intercourse, so the case of a rape could not be confirmatively made out. No evidence was available. However, further investigations were ordered", added Manorama.

"I want your readings. What is it that you have to say regarding the matter?", questioned Ram Kumar.

"Well, I could. If you are willing to open your ears and listen. And of course, even if I were to give you the true facts, would it help matters? Can you do something about it? In fact do you even want to? If yes, then I may disclose the facts", Manorma minced no words.

"Yes, why ever the hell not?", Ram Kumar reacted to the instigation.

"Nay, I don't want mere superficial assurances. There is no one who will give any evidence here. There are inter-tribal rivalries, a desperate race for survival, every living thing here is struggling for its own survival. Then the place is infested with insurgent gangs and one of these gangs has become a holy terror in this area. People cringe at the mere mention of this gang."

"What? No one will give evidence because of the fear of the insurgents?"

"On the contrary it is the police and administration here, who have been callously exploiting the poor tribals. People here are totally disillusioned by those that claim to be their saviors, the so called protectors of law. So they have gradually turned to the insurgents. These are the groups that have offered to protect the tribals from all external threats and they help to settle their internal disputes. So the tribal here has more faith in the official crime breaker than in the official protector. You see what I mean.....", Manorama stopped mid sentence.

"That is shocking!"

"Indeed, so it is! And mind you, it has not been so because of a dearth of visits from many officials. They also came with several new schemes. But none were really implemented. The contractors working in these areas quietly hand over 25% commission to the insurgents while the officials and the politicians of the area have their own individual rates. What is even more appalling is the fact that the government officials themselves, under pretext of the names of the different groups of insurgents, are walking away with the king's slice of the pie. So everybody has their cut in the pie, but then what about the common man? What about them? Since this area has been officially declared as 'disturbed', therefore, large contingents of forces are being deputed here. The entire region is flooded with them, and mind you, these so called protectors too don't spare the common man. They demand their share indeed."

"Don't tell me, is that really happening here?", came a disgusted reaction from Ram Kumar.

"Oh yes! We have all the departments making a neat income in the name of the so called villains of the land, the insurgents. The Police will do just about anything in the name of their operations", opined Manorama.

"Your words smack of revolutionary ideas", Kumar interrupted.

"Well I am really not surprised. I can vouch that if you were to spend a few years amidst these conditions you'd be voicing the same thoughts", was Manorama's reaction.

It was past two o'clock in the afternoon. The orderly appeared in the doorway and quietly announced that lunch was laid out in the Inspection Bungalow. Ram Kumar politely invited Manorama to join him for lunch.

"I have had an early meal, you go ahead please", Manorama politely declined the offer.

As he was leaving, Ram Kumar noticed a few tribals sitting, crouched close outside the police chowki. He felt like getting down from his vehicle to talk to them, but the moment passed him as the car cruised past. He wirelessed the Inspector Incharge of the Chowki to inform the group that he would return to their village and would visit them at 4 o'clock in the evening and hear out their problems.

Manorama, in the meanwhile, had stopped to speak to the group of tribals. She noticed Ketaki amongst them. She reprimanded her gently, "You have again bunked class. Why were you not there yesterday?"

"Mai, my child was very unwell, he would not leave me. He had been crying a lot."

"Oh I see! You should have brought him along. Next time bring him along with you. I will help you manage him," reassured Manorama. So saying, Manorama approached Ketaki and casually pulled up her tattered blouse, which hid much less then what it exposed. The embarrassed sub-inspector, who had been looking their way, uncomfortably looked away.

"It's unfortunate that these people have little to cover them. You, I hope, are here to help them. But I am afraid you are not noticing what you really need to see. I hope you have some self respect and will put in some effort to keep your image high at least in your own eyes," Manorama looked deep into the Inspector's bespectacled eyes and then looking pointedly at his name plate, quickly rose and left the room.

Mr. Ram Kumar arrived in the village sharply at 4 o'clock. He was obviously a man who valued time.

There were about ten to twelve 'Bashas' (huts made of dried bamboo sticks and coconut leaves). Midway there was a rectangular area where a hand pump that had dried out stood as a mute witness to the helpless state of the inhabitants around. Hearing the noise of the car wheels coming to a screeching halt just outside, some of the occupants of the bashas could be seen peeping out of their doors, gradually filtering out to watch with vacant expressions the approaching group led by Ram Kumar.

He entered the last basha. The hut was dark, dingy. It took a good few minutes for his eyes to get acclimatized to the dark. Gradually, he noticed an old withered man crouched in a corner. He sat there unmoving, almost as if he was a wax figure, not a breathing human. He was literally an emaciated skeletal frame who sat there with his knees bent, digging into his ribs and his feet were caked with mud that seemed to have settled on it gradually over several days.

The old man noticing the intrusion, cringed as if expecting the land revenue officer to have descended on them once again. "Sir, this man is completely insane", butted in the local sub-inspector who had accompanied Kumar.

"No, that is a lie. Good afternoon Sahib", a stern voice reacted from the depths of the hutment. Ram Kumar looked closely. A middle aged man, Matadin, greeted him. "I am working along with Manoramaji", explained Matadin.

"Where is your madam?"

"She will be here any minute sahib."

"Oh I see! You reacted to the sub-inspector's comment, did you not?', queried Kumar.

"Sir, the old man here is not mad. However, he has been declared to be so. The poor man has been awaiting to get back the possession of his land for the past twenty years. A land, which had been promised to him by a land revenue officer, who had assured him that he would get his land back. But, not surprisingly, his applications have been buried and lost under the piles of files. Look at the irony of fate! The administration did nothing to help him to recover his land that had been snatched away by some rich goons with a lot of clout in this area. Instead they have declared him mentally unstable so that they do not even have to bother to entertain his repeated pleadings", informed Matadin.

"Does he have no other family?", queried Kumar.

"Yes, he does have a daughter, 'Ketaki'. She has a child too. However, her husband has been put behind bars based on the allegation that he is an ally of the insurgents," informed Matadin.

Ram Kumar could take it no longer. It was easy to take decisions on paper but to see them implemented in real life was a different story altogether. He felt drained, it was pointless. The miasmas were too deep rooted. They had gradually spread their tentacles through out society. It was next to impossible to try and end it. With a heavy heart he gradually trudged back to the car, absent-mindedly returning the eager greetings of the hungry, expectant faces now queing in line to greet the bada sahib.

That evening he called the district officials to his Rest House. Manorama was also invited.

"Sir, if you should allow, may I put a question to our revered district S.P.?", Manorama had made a pertinent remark that was framed behind a question.

"Why not, please, by all means."

"My information says that the mass rapes are the doings of a few surrendered insurgents in connivance with a few of our own cops."

"How dare you make such an allegation?", the S.P. reacted violently.

"Through very reliable sources, you know. After all only a criminal knows the inside story of another and only a cop can tell something about another cop", enlightened Manorama.

The S.P. turned an ashen white. He had had a whiff of the goings on but he had not dared to verify the facts. After a moment's lapse, he mildly reacted, in a shaken under tone, "If that should be true, I can assure you no guilty shall be spared."

What needed to be said had already been said, so the meeting ended very soon after.

The S.P. returned fuming within. He immediately called for his Deputy S.P. (Operations) and chided him, "I have been informed through reliable sources that some of our CATS along with some of our soldiers are involved in this case of mass rape of the tribal women. If that is so, God help you. I am giving you time till tomorrow to find the truth", warned the S.P. Realising that he was cornered, the Dy. SP (Ops) J.D. Singh confessed with his head hung in shame, "Sir some of our own people are responsible for these rapes. I could never have dreamed in my wildest dreams that these bastards would stoop to this extent...."

"Mind your language, Singh", warned the SP. "You may leave."

Next morning it was publicly declared that an FIR had been registered against the group of CATS and the Cops involved in the crime. The case then was handed over to the CID. The case remained canned and gradually people forgot about the happening.

But the two vital characters of this tale still live on.

Manorama today is a frail reminder of her earlier bubbly self. She is well aware of what had eventually happened. The CATS had been killed in an encounter by the cops and there was no witness who came up to give evidence on the later dates.

Manorama was a crest fallen women. She felt she had failed in her mission to bring justice to the downtrodden. She blamed herself for her failings. Her health gradually failed too, till she was forced to remain restricted within the four walls of her house.

Ketakii, came in the evening as usual to administer Manorama's medicines to her and to press her weak, aching feet. Manorama brought up that case and expressed her helplessness to help Ketaki retrieve her land.

"Mai, you have already done so much for our lot. You are the only one who has fought for our cause. Infact, if it were not for you, may be today I would not be here, I never told you, that night even I was ra..... Ketaki's eyelids moistened as she spoke. Slowly her tears began to fall. They fell one after the other on Manorama's feet. Manorama felt the frustration burning up her insides, the tears fell like scalding coals taunting her further at her failures. Unable to bear it any further, Manorama murmured, "Go home Ketaki, I cannot do anything for you."

Ketaki sprang up and rushed out, running all the way to her hut where her father still remained seated, rooted to the same spot in the hidden corner of the hut. Angry at her helplessness, Ketaki spewed venom, "Why don't you die. I have stashed away fifty rupees for your last rites. Someone must die. I cannot even die. I have this brat to feed. So I must slowly burn, consumed along with the charred bamboos".

Just then a rough nasal voice boomed from outside the hut, "O Ketaki, come". Ketaki sat there mute and unresponding. The hungry male voice repeated its vulgar calling a few more times and then came the sound of the retreating footsteps. There were other willing doors that would open today. Ketaki alone did not carry the sole rights to human merchandise.

* * *

Chapter 17

SUICIDE

He lay there in a pool of blood. He had always been a family man, a man whose priorities had only been the well being of his family, their welfare, and their comforts. To him the term 'family' meant not just his wife but his parents too. Only he had known what it had meant for him to walk away from them, leaving them behind to fend for themselves. He always carried a deep noted sense of guilt that he had not been able to do for them what he had dreamt. The urge to please them had been one of the major factors for which he had applied for this job in the Forces. He had imagined his family preening over his accomplishments. He had dreamt of the stars and the medals that would adorn his chest making them so proud of him that whatever ways he may have failed them in his adolescent years would be forgotten, his earlier sins washed away. He had imagined the devil had been finally laid to rest. He had gone another step further and married a simple, plain girl of his parent's choice. Yet, what had driven him to this? This violent end. Did he deserve it, what could have lead to it?

He lay there, cold and lifeless, his eyes remained wide open. A glassy look had now replaced the expected actions in them.

The bullet that had killed him had pierced through his throat at an awkward angle of forty five degrees and passed through the head and then hit the ground with immense impact. It had then ricocheted and made a final entry into the wall facing the door at about a height of four feet above the ground.

For some time, the verifying squad remained bewildered - was it a murder or a suicide, various premiss were worked upon, possibilities explored and deductions made. Several senior officers visited the scene of the mishap. In most likelihood the Head Constable, Rajeshwar Singh, had committed suicide.

And this was finally confirmed when a suicide note was recovered from the back pocket of one of the trousers hanging from the hook on the side wall. The room had actually been a dingy store room placed in the rear of the main building. Due to a shortage of accommodation space it had been converted into his living quarters. He slept here alone.

Just the night before he had last been seen around 2230 hrs, after which he had left the local telephone booth from where he had made repeated phone calls to his family.

The local police had confiscated the gun that had been in the Head Constable Rajeshwar's possession. The position in which the gun had been recovered, the entry and the exit points made by the bullet on Rajeshwar's body, the adjoining area and the floor was all very carefully cordoned off to prevent people from erasing any evidence and then carefully photographed in extensive detail. Sketches were also carefully drawn and developed to provide further leads. The likely time, exact hour was carefully determined. It took over two to three hours to decide on the likely chain of events.

Finally, the body was deported for a detailed postmortem. The message was forwarded to all the senior formations stating that the evidence till then indicated it being a clear case of suicide.

The officers had heaved a sigh of relief. At least, the fellow had not gone ahead and committed suicide because of any act of official omission or negligence like a denial of leave and the like. It had been due to personal reasons. The deceased had several family issues that had obviously driven him to take such a drastic step.

The routine official disposal of the matter was soon over but it did not satisfy Narendra Bharadwaj, the Deputy Inspector General of the area who visited the unit and went through the papers minutely. He was a man who did not believe in taking half baked measures and would not give up looking into the matter till he was convinced that the symptoms that had surfaced were not being confused for being the disease itself.

Something bothered him, something was not quite right He knew they were missing out on some vital facts and he wanted to get to the heart of the reasons.

So, he began interacting personally with the different unit members. Rajeshwar's friends and associates were personally interrogated by him extensively. He even went to the extent of speaking individually on the phone to each of Rajeshwar's family members.

Then, it soon came to light that according to the records that were maintained at the local PCO, Rajeshwar had spoken to his wife thrice in the evening at an interval of about half an hour, then ten minutes, followed by another immediate call within a gap of not more than five minutes. The duration of the calls also followed a similar pattern.

It was quite clear now that something had upset Rajeshwar, some pressing concern had been bothering him, causing him to make repeated calls back home within a short duration of time.

Bhardwaj's next step was to get in touch with those people who had been at that time in the PCO immediately behind Rajeshwar waiting for their turn to make their calls.

It was discovered that Rajeshwar had been in the booth for close to an hour. Some of the frustrated callers in waiting had finally ventured inside the booth to coax him to cut short his conversation. These intermittent interceptors confirmed that every time they had overheard him desperately trying to persuade his wife to immediately hand over Rupees fifteen thousand to his father in connection with the freeing of some land. Any further details could not be made available.

Next, Bharadwaj worked on Rajeshwar's contacts. Rajeshwar's best friend, Chandra Mohan gave further clues.

Persistent discrete enquiries and interrogations finally egged on to reveal that there were deep inbuilt simmering tensions brewing amongst the soldiers of the forces that were deployed for long spells in far away, remote insurgency prone areas. Rajeshwar too was one of the victims. Lately, he had been showing some signs of depression. He was desperate to take leave and go home.

In fact, it soon emerged that Rajeshwar had some time back finalised a deal for a piece of land in order to construct his own house in his home village. He had already made an advance payment of Rupees One lac to this effect.

But unfortunately, his being away in the north east districts on duty made it really difficult for him to follow up on this matter in his hometown at Pratapgarh in Uttar Pradesh.

Poor Rajeshwar's repeated pleas to the local authorities fell on deaf ears. They refused to pay heed to his submissions. In the meantime, the original owner sold the piece of land to another lucrative purchaser. There was another complication too in this deal. Rajeshwar had been falling short of money and had therefore borrowed forty thousand rupees from his father in order to enable him to pay for that piece of land.

Since the deal had fallen through, so his father who had been going through difficult times asked Rajeshwar to repay the money. This was Chandra Mohan's briefing to Bharadwaj before the latter intercepted him, "You mean to say the failure of the land deal to go across was the reason behind his committing suicide. This, I am afraid appears to be a little far fetched. And after all, as far as the money that he had borrowed from his father was concerned, he could always return the money to his father in instalments."

"No sir, it was not as simple as that. Rajeshwar had committed to his old father that he would return the borrowed amount in three installments. It was to begin with the first installment of an amount of rupees fifteen thousand. He sent this amount to his wife with clear-cut instructions that it was to be handed over to his father. But his wife put a spanner in his plans. She clearly let him know that she was disinclined to handover the sum to his father, stating that she did not see what was the urgency of the money to be passed on to his father, immediately. According to her there were far more pressing issues with her that needed to be attended to, so instead she utilised the money to purchase miscellaneous items for the household which she had been wanting to purchase for a very long time", Chandra Mohan continued to disclose the sequence of events.

"But if he was going through a crisis, you could have offered to help, you were supposedly his very close friend", chided Bharadwaj.

"Why should you suppose, Sir, that I did not attempt to help him out. I gave him moral and material support to the best of my abilities. We had even withdrawn money from our provident fund.

Rajeshwar realised that his father was too weak and old to fend for himself. So, he was anxious to return the money. We had somehow amassed the fifteen thousand rupees and the fact that his wife refused to handover the money to his father burdened him with an immense sense of guilt.

Then, on the other hand, his wife was still not satisfied. She was constantly nagging him, badgering him constantly about how he neglected her, how he was an imbecile, a beast with no fine sentiments, with no consideration for her needs, her wants. She felt very wronged. She also complained that their marriage was pointless, he was hardly there with her; he spent barely two months of a year at home. She felt she was merely playing the role of his housemaid, managing his house and the problems that came along with it. In other words, Rajeshwar was a man constantly harassed and stressed out", Chandra Mohan spoke out what he knew about his friend's family life.

"It is really unfortunate that Rajesh was unable to deal with his personal pressures and for a mere sum of fifteen thousand rupees he ended his life", sympathised Bharadwaj.

"No sir, not really. This was or could at best be the igniting point that drove the man to his death. Insurgency prone areas have their own complex issues; high security risks restrict our free movements. Heavy duty agendas hardly leave us with anytime to attend to our personal issues, our families, our homes. Then mobile phones, though a definite facility, are not without its cons, as it brings along with it to us the daily tensions of our families. Strict regimentation in our force kills all the avenues of vertical interaction. Sir, there are hardly any officers like you in the force. We have felt free to talk to you, to discuss our issues with you. But, this is generally not the case". Chandra Mohan wanted to elaborate further but he was forced to stop as Bharadwaj had got up and moved to a far corner. He was obviously deep in thought, brooding over some serious matter. Chandra Mohan had no inkling what it was that had caught his boss's attention.

But Bharadwaj could finally see the light at the end of the tunnel. He felt that if they handled the issue well, some of these issues could be successfully dealt with. If only Rajeshwar had felt the confidence to freely talk out his issues, they would not have lost a fine solider.

He realised that they were not providing an environment where the soldiers could relate and talk over their issues with a sympathetic senior. Were they really not providing an environment where they listened patiently with an open mind to deal with personal issues individually? If only 'dialogue' avenues could be left open and our ears receptive.

Then the 'rebel' that is dormant in each individual would not find outlets in brutality and destructive measures. Our rationale would then provide us with sensible resolves.

At times mere listening through our eyes would communicate much more than our ears could.

'Is anyone listening?'

* * *

Chapter 18

SHOOT OUT

It was just past five o'clock on a hot summer evening when a burst of AK-47 in the camp of a police post sent a flurry of confused activity in its entire vicinity.

The initial reaction all around was that the camp had been attacked by insurgents. A frantic message was flashed across the police net. Since the camp was located only a stones throw away from the town Dampura, the near by police units were immediately galvanised into action and rushed in to help. Smelling a rat, the media too arrived for a detailed coverage.

The Commanding Officer, who had been away on some business, was directed to immediately return to the camp by the Inspector General who also had been camping in the district headquarters. The local police too reached the spot in no time and got down to work, verifying the source of the attack. Very soon, it was established without an iota of doubt that it had not been an external attack. Something had gone seriously wrong within the camp premises but it was yet to be determined 'What'!

The wireless post within the camp which had been disrupted was quickly repaired. It then relayed the happening – five police personnel including the platoon commander had been shot dead by another constable of the platoon, Sukhvinder Singh. He was still in possession of the gun and after the shoot out he had taken cover in a 'morcha' constructed within the camp to attack the enemy. The remaining platoon had immediately taken their positions to cover him.

The Commandant of the company, Vijay, had in the meantime reached the camp too. He quickly, along with a few of Sukhvinder's good friends in the camp, was now stealthily approaching the morcha all the while keeping Sukhvinder engaged, his attention distracted, with urgings of a reconciliation, "You know Sukhvinder yaar, you've always been my trusted soldier. I shall never leave you in the lurch. You are a son to me, I have trusted you. I shall continue to trust you, I cannot harm you, son, but you are free to hit me. So I'm coming to you now". Vijay was moving closer. In the meantime he had given explicit orders to the rest of his personnel not to open fire on Sukhvinder.

Obviously, man continues to be a slave of his emotions. Visibly moved Sukhvinder came out from behind the morcha holding his gun high above his head. The arms and ammunitions were taken away from him. An agitated Comrade gave vent to his pent up fury but Vijay, an old hand, prevented him. Vijay's foremost concern was to extract the full facts from Sukhvinder while he was in this vulnerable state of mind. Torture needed to be an eventual resort only when all other methods failed.

Taking Sukhvinder's friends into confidence he convinced them to help him in succeeding to break him down emotionally.

Gradually, Sukhvinder opened up. He agreed to disclose what exactly had transpired that had prompted him to take such a drastic step.

At this stage Vijay noticed from the corner of his eyes that some of the onlookers who had curiously assembled to feast on the goings on, now could be seen quietly slinking away under some pretext or the other.

Vijay's mind was now working overtime. Probably, these people had something to hide, they were afraid of what it was, that Sukhvinder was about to disclose. Obviously these were not mere curious innocent bystanders. They had had a role to play too in this terrible death dance.

Feigning to comment yet on his perceptions, Vijay continued to direct his staff to have the area vacated as he wished to talk to Sukhvinder separately in greater detail without any disturbance. He was well aware that the presence of a crowd around them would only hamper their progress and it may even prevent Sukhvinder from unwinding and communicating. It could have a serious adverse impact on him, preventing him from confiding in Vijay. He was well aware that for the time being Vijay had managed to win his complete confidence. The details that Sukhvinder gradually unfolded spoke volumes of the traumatizing factors that the security personnel are subjected to. It could be the hostile unfriendly environment in which they are forced to survive for long spells in distant places, far removed from their families and friends; it could be the result of the constant threat to life, watching people die day in day out as a matter of routine; it could be the gradual erosion of their sensitivities in these sub-optimal surroundings that these people are forced to live in, which in turn, may lead to their emotional bankruptcy.

It may actually take a team of psychoanalysts several years to ascertain the time variables that are acting as an impetus to such fallouts.

Vijay did not wish to waste any further time, therefore he ensured that a comfortable and protective environment be offered to Sukhvinder in order to encourage him to reveal the sordid happening and the causes that had build up to it. At regular intervals Vijay provided the much needed emotional strokes.

Gradually, it started to pour out till all had tumbled out from the deep recesses of Sukhvinders mental cupboard. The venom, the pain, the frustration, the terror and the pent up fury – he gave vent to it all.

"Sir, I did not even want to harm them, let alone kill them. But they humiliated me and that too before the local girls. They called me the 'na-mard'. They said I was impotent", Sukhvinder broke down.

"What, that is no reason to shoot down a person. They may have been just joking" was Vijay's incredulous reaction.

"Sir, it has been a long drawn out miserable existence for me. They have humiliated me repeatedly. I have suffered it all in silence so far", Sukhvinder implored.

"Just what is he trying to say?" Vijay looked perplexed while targetting the question at the Company Commander. The Company Commander Gurdeep had been trying to avoid making any comment on the issue.

"No sir, not him, please don't get me wrong. He has been extremely good to me. Infact, he is the only person who has been nice to me in this unit", Sukhvinder was pleading Gurdeep's case.

Sensing Gurdeep's involvement too in the matter, Vijay could now feel an irritation building up in him. Gurdeep had been a party to it all along and yet he had chosen to keep Vijay in the dark. This could not be forgiven. It was a breach of faith and would need suitable chastisement.

"I don't understand. Gurdeep, did you know about the development? Have you been keeping information from me" , Vijay was in no mood to forgive now.

"Sir, I must confess, I have for sometime known about Sukhvinder's issues. But this has come as a total surprise to me too, sir. Today's developments have been sporadic. All the three, whose comments sparked off the shoot out, are lying dead", informed Gurdeep.

"I confess that I could bear their digs, their constant jibes no more. I wanted to kill them, but only these three, the other two just came in between the shots. I am now ready to tell you sir my entire story", confessed Sukhwinder.

"Go ahead then'" prompted Vijay.

"Sir, it began when I was posted with a unit in Manipur. There somebody spread a canard that I had contracted AIDS. In fact, I did have a serious problem but of a different nature. My wife had left me because of some other issues and was living with her parents. There she discovered she was carrying my child. On getting the news I was ecstatic, forgetting our recent differences I wanted to rush down and be by her side, but they refused my leave. I could only visit her after 4-5 months. This delay had been perceived by her and her family as a clear show of my callousness. Hence, when I arrived, no welcome faces greeted me. In fact, they humiliated me and told me to go back. I somehow returned, a broken man", confessed Sukhvinder with tears filling up his eyes.

Vijay warmed up to him and patted his shoulder in reassurance, "Don't lose heart, we are with you now, you are not alone. We shall help you get through. Tell us what happened thereafter."

"I went home again after a few days. Unfortunately, I decided to take Amrinder along, one of those who I killed today, as he was on leave and belonged to the village right next to mine. I had taken him along to provide proof to my wife that I was stating the truth, when I had informed them that I had been denied leave, Amrinder further reassured my love and affections for my wife and for my child. But my wife refused to accept his pleas and in her agitated state of mind and her need to hurt me further declared in the presence of Amrinder and the others, "This is not your child." It was difficult to contain Sukhvinder, as he sobbed unabashedly.

Gurdeep proceeded to fetch him a glass of water which he took and gulped down slowly. Collecting himself he continued further, "I returned to the unit. But here, on return, my miseries worsened. Amrinder had spread the word that the child my wife was carrying was not mine. I had become the butt of ridicule in my entire unit. They sniggered behind my back. Things worsened further when somebody added another canard that my wife had deserted me as I had AIDS.

So desperate was I to prove my innocence that I got myself tested to prove that I did not have AIDS. But the jokes, the sniggers, the jibes, the taunts continued unabated. Gurdeep was the only one to sympathise sir", Sukhwinder placed his right hand into his pocket and drew out a crumbled report handing it to Vijay in a touching attempt to prove his innocence even now.

Vijay could just look into Sukhvinder's eyes sharing his pain. He looked like a lost child looking for some help to guide him back to the safe climes of his homeland.

"This ugly tale was also conveyed back home to my wife who then wanted nothing further to do with me. I was not allowed long leave to go home to set things right and remove those misunderstandings as I had already exhausted all my leave. My home is very far from here. Constant stress and tension had already begun to take its toll on me and to top it all, these guys stood there at the gate openly deriding me, calling me the most inconceivable names and that too in front of these local girls. My threshold could bear the brunt no further. These girls whom Amrinder and the group had befriended had become regular visitors, coming here to the camp under the pretext of selling shawls. I could not bear the humiliation day in day out and now to be called a 'na-mard' before these girls. It had become impossible to contain the tide of anger that was threatening to explode within me. Something within me snapped. I had eaten humble pie long enough. My self-respect was not ready to be trampled upon any further. For them it was a vicious joke, for me it was my life at stake. They had ruined me, they had taken away my purpose of survival and I have taken away theirs. The bandh within me broke. I did what I wanted to do and I candidly admit that I feel no repentance for my doing. I should have probably done this long back. But the pansy within me refused to retaliate. I know they will send me to jail, may be even hang me. I know my life is finished. I will not get to see my wife, my child. But at least I am a 'mard' and I shall live with that."

But the story does not end here. It is not just one Sukhvinder's tale. Perhaps mishaps and misunderstandings are a common place occurrence that in turn give rise to diverse formats of insurgencies in personal lives too.

As an observer, one can comment, "if only tackled carefully and sensitively, so many conflict situations can be avoided".

* * *

Chapter 19

THE INCENTIVE

Tea garden estates in Assam have long been a flourishing industry. The estate owners enjoy an ostentatious life style, live in opulent bungalows with huge sprawling gardens. In other words, they enjoy all the benefits and comforts of a magnificent life.

The distant hillocks covered with a thick green foliage, lush expanses of tea bushes, winding water rivulets all combine to lay bare to the naked eye, a scenic sight that seems to have slipped right out of a picture book.

But then, suddenly everything changed drastically. The terrible sounds of gun shots replaced the musical lilting chords of the surroundings that had so far strung the local people's hearts. So great was the fear of violence that all movements would come to a stand still once the sun had set. Initially, even the police forces restricted their movements. A few of them even removed the official insignias. Gradually, the destructive fire of insurgency engulfed the entire area. The rich owners of the tea estates and the tea garden managers became the prime targets of kidnapping and extortion.

Even the police force was not adequately reinforced to meet these new challenges posed by the violent and 'explosive-equipped' groups.

This incident belongs to those very days, just about a decade back when insurgency had begun to surface and had taken a violent turn.

In the early hours of the morning a message was relayed across on the police wireless network, "Six people including the manager of the Mohan tea estate have been kidnapped by the local insurgent group. SHO of the district is on a hot chase in the direction of their retreat."

The local SP of that district, Tinsukhia, immediately got in touch with his officers and the Commandant of the reserve battalion that had been camping in that district for sometime.

The additional SP did not have a very promising picture to project, "Sir, the area involved is unwieldy and vast. I have very carefully studied the length and breadth of the region. We shall need a strength of ten companies along with at least a dozen officers to monitor and successfully comb the entire area, if we intend to take the insurgents head on. After all, we need to ensure the safety of those who have been kidnapped too."

"Okay, let us see", the SP pondered a while and then made his decision, "divert all the forces from the city pickets and withdraw the men from garrison duties. Carefully divide the parties, clearly demarcating the areas they are to cover and make a distinct distribution of their duties. Also, make sure that you have first finalised how the different parties shall approach their zones, what procedures they are to follow for effective coordination, the passwords and the required codes also need to be finalised and shared. You go ahead and do the needful while I shall join you immediately after I have informed the higher ups."

The Second-in-Command nodded in agreement. The additional SP gave a detailed briefing to the bold and the able officers of the battalion to lead their respective teams. They put their heads together and finalised the plans. The whole procedure took about an hour. In this time, the ordered forces had also moved in from the various positions.

As the afternoon approached, the entire area had been sealed off and the parties positioned at crucial points. A few local conversant people were left free to roam in the area so that the sheltering haunts of the insurgents could be traced. Their possible shelters and nearby areas, covering an expanse of about 120 Sq. Kms. including some shallow valleys, and a few dotted hutments were encircled. After a lapse of about 3-4 hours the news filtered in that two of the six kidnapped had been recovered as they were abandoned because of their inability to walk across the harsh terrain. Then came the information from another source that the kidnappers had been traced along with the four remaining kidnapped persons, hiding in a small discrepit hutment about seven Kms away on the periphery of the village numbered 'Ten'.

Unfortunately, by the time the police could reach the spot the insurgents had deserted the spot. However, careful interrogation of the hutments' owners revealed that they were in all 8 of them, 4 of the kidnapped were accompanied by 4 insurgents. The kidnappers were equipped with AK-47, self loading rifles and a handful of grenades.

Immediately beyond the hutment flowed a thin rivulet that snaked across the area following the gradient of the terrain. The party on duty across the rivulet, however, sent forth the information that this party of 'eight' had not been sighted across the stream.

The District SP along with his advisors decided, and wisely so, that it made sense to concentrate their force all along the stream, particularly around the area where the water was shallow and most easily accessible. Even those on night duty were sternly ordered to stay on the alert. "No laxity on your part will be tolerated", barked their Commandant.

The night hours eased along and finally came day break with no signs of the eight being traced. However, the one encouraging sign was that the parties that had been combing the area in the morning had detected fresh footprints along the riverbed. This was a clear indication that their had been some human movement in the dark hours of the night. The SP, when informed of this, was livid. He hollered at the party commander, "Do you take me for an imbecile! How in heavens is it possible to find fresh footprints there and you claim there has been no movement in your area?" But the Commandant stuck to the story that his men had been on a very strict vigil and no movement could possibly have occurred while they were on duty.

The SP was beginning to feel increasingly more frustrated. Just then he noticed one of the constables on duty trying very hard not to meet his eyes. The S.P. noticed that the man kept looking his way and then away again. He sensed that the man wanted to say something to him but was afraid to do so in the open. So he took him aside and spoke to him encouraging him to narrate the facts without any hitch.

"Sir, I want to tell you, but I am afraid....."

The SP intervened, "Don't be. Even if it has been a lapse, we shall try and improve upon it for the future!"

"Sir, we had seen them cross the river in the middle of the night."

"So, why did you all do nothing to prevent them?"

"Sir, our Party incharge, Mr. Naresh, prevented us from doing so."

The SP looked in Naresh's direction, who had all this while maintained a studied silence.

But now he spoke, "Sir, that is right. But, then at that hour I felt that it would be prudent to keep my men from reacting. You see, as you are well aware, our party only had .303 rifles. If we had missed our targets, their AK-47's, their SLRs, would have in no time made mince meat of all my people. My conscience dictated otherwise. And as their commander, I thought it wise not to expose them to any unnecessary threat to life. After all they are my moral responsibility".

Naresh had put his case across well. The SP realised why his force had failed him. He ordered for the force to collect for a briefing.

"Look, we are the official protectors of public life and property. When we don our uniform, along with that we take the oath to lay down our lives for the sake of the security of our people. There may be times when we may find ourselves wanting in arms and ammunitions. We may lack the apparatus but we are not wanting in intellect, in strategic planning and in guts. We shall win our battles with whatever limited resources we have at our beck and call."

The officers and constables supportingly raised their hands and nodded in agreement.

'No, not just this. We first need to have the firm commitment that there is no other way but to win. We have to win. We are in no way inferior to these rogues. We have the self respect to fight off this scourge of our society. Do we return to our home and hearth and tell our children that we were outwitted by these rascals and so beat a quick retreat?", chided the SP.

Visibly moved, the force reacted "Sir, enough, we feel ashamed. Please stop! No more sir, we have realised our mistake. It shall not happen again. We are ready for fresh action", Naresh appeared to be visibly chastened.

But the SP was not yet done with them. He continued, "If one's morale is high, nothing can stand in our way. Don't we all know of those instances where the weak built, mild farmers, villagers with no arms, no reinforcements have pelted to death with stones, the dacoits that threatened their villages and families. Therefore, please I expect your solemn assurance that yesterday's folly shall not to be repeated ever again". The meeting now stood adjourned.

There could be noticed a visible change in the police camp. Action thrived, plans were implemented. The force got lucky sooner then they had expected. The gang's position was tapped. Heavy firing followed from both sides. Naresh's helper was hit on the neck by a bullet that pierced killing him on the spot. But Naresh stood his ground unfazed. He continued firing, because now his mind was made up, his target was within his reach and his mission clear. It was eventually his bullets that fell two of the four insurgents.

Meanwhile, the range DIG had reached a tea estate's guest house right on the periphery of the forested area where intense combing was being conducted. He demanded of his SP the details of the goings on. On the SP's briefing of how Naresh and his men had, on the earlier night, missed an opportunity to nab the kidnappers, the DIG lost his temper and ordered Naresh's immediate suspension.

"Sir, I have already giving him a sufficient dressing down. He has been apologetic and I can vouch now that he shall not fail us in the future. Kindly spare him this time", pleaded the SP.

"Cowardice in police official is unforgivable", roared the DIG. "Sir, I don't completely hold him responsible for his inaction. Our weapons are old and outdated. Our parties are not even equipped with adequate protective gears and vests. And above all they lack the training for counter insurgency operations", the SP was doing his best to protect Naresh and his men. After all, Naresh had proved his mettle in several earlier operations. The man had caliber and the SP had realised that good and proper. Such officers were rare to come across in the forces.

"Since, you insist! But if such an irresponsible happening should repeat itself, it shall be your head on the chopping board," declared an obviously disgruntled DIG. The SP left immediately to join his team members. He was determined that he would prove to his peers and superiors that his men were able, efficient and brave men, capable of tackling any adversity or threat.

The scene in the action zone was gradually turning favourable. After losing two of their colleagues the remaining kidnappers began to lose their nerve. They had also received some injuries. The kidnapped, taking advantage of the distractions, managed to escape. The injured kidnappers crawled some distance and hid behind some stray dense growth.

The guns fell silent for sometime. Then Naresh and his men gradually inched their way to the dead kidnappers. They counted the two heads. That meant two of them were still on the prowl. Naresh noticed a bloody trail leading at some distance into the dense growth nearby. The remaining two surrendered soon without offering any resistance. They were critically injured and in no state to further the battle.

Naresh's eyes were searching for his SP. And he did not have to look very far. The SP had reached the spot and his eyes looked upon Naresh with a new found respect and deep affection. Naresh felt a sense of gratitude sweep over him. Tears of relief trailed down his cheeks. He declared proudly, "Sir I am not a coward!"

The SP nodded his assent and said, "Naresh, I am recommending your case for a gallantry medal".

But Naresh resisted, "No sir, we are paid to serve our people. We don't need any added incentives to perform our duty." Naresh felt self-actualised. He now needed no medals, no recommendations, no applaudings!

There were scores of praises that now filtered in on Naresh's achievement. But a few still expressed reservations and asked the SP, 'Was the encounter by any chance a fake?" The SP resisted the urge to react sharply. He wanted to admonish them for belittling this grand feat. But was it their fault really. The Police is infamous for its false encounters. So no wonder people doubt even the genuine ones. He turned and smiled benignly, "Take it, as you should presume", and he walked away from the scene.

* * *

Chapter 20

REFLECTIONS OF A COP

I remember long back somebody had asked, "Suppose you had to write your own obituary to be read out after your death, what would you write?" I laughingly let the remark pass off.

But, today, when I am an old doddering foggy at the fag end of my life, my past often niggles me forcing my tears to brim over. My conscience rebukes me often, "Time is running out for you Anand. Is there any positive action of your past that you can proudly announce to the world?"

My past races across. I recollect, how brimming with excitement and confidence I was, after having completed my studies. I had gotten selected as a class one gazetted officer with the government of India. Then after completing my formal training sincerely, I commenced my service with dignity. However, when I looked for legal structures within the grand realities, law became an illusive term both in letter as well as in spirit. Then, there surfaced many advisors amidst varying pulls and pressures. It took me sometime and some startling experiences that eventually taught me 'How to be practical'!

I still remember very distinctly, I had gone to a nearby village for an official visit. The people there had many local disputes that needed to be settled. Being a young enthusiastic officer raring to go in a newly acquired position, I took my job very seriously. So I decided to camp at the village for a week to deliver results. I did get positive response. I returned with a deep sense of satisfaction that I could bring back the smile on the faces of many of these simple downtrodden folks. I had managed to successfully resolve their problems, the problems that had festered through the ages.

But what awaited me, when I returned, completely perplexed me. On my return to the headquarters my seniors rebuked me, commenting, "you are on a job you know, not a picnic. If you need to relax, you may kindly proceed on leave..." The chiding stunned me. On one end were the grateful blessings of the villagers and in complete contrast was this reaction of his seniors.

My immediate boss, however, had begun to understand me by then. Realising that he was the only somewhat sympathetic ear I had, I unloaded my tale of woe before him, of how I had slogged untiringly for three whole days living in an extremely frugal setting with a committed effort to resolve those long pending issues of the villagers. These were villagers who could not possibly afford to knock at the door of the judicial courts. My boss appreciated my effort but he also had a piece of advice for me – "you cannot serve the people unless whatever it is that you do for them, you ensure that it is sufficiently propagated. Also learn to hold the ropes fast and start cultivating those people who are in the saddle, if you really want to go places in your career. Else be prepared to stagnate".

I was slowly picking up the ropes and gradually changing my work style. But today when I look back, I realise that I had felt the greatest happiness when I had done what I did for the villagers in those three memorable days, while many of the later events of my life, when I had worked at placating those 'people of substance', gave me no enduring satisfaction. I realise today that only those moments had healed me which I had spent helping others selflessly.

I still recall the advise of those so called 'well-wishers'. Their advice had been to me, "Better work at getting hold of a God-father, a strong anchor will facilitate your postings and provide you a conducive work environment". Initially, I had paid no heed. Gradually I waivered, watching my peers as their influence gradually began to wear off on me too, and I began to see some benefits in it. It meant important postings. Lobbying amidst influential people did lead to momentary accomplishments and happiness, it temporarily satiated my ego but then very soon I realised the futility of what I was indulging in. The temporary nature of the importance that came along with these lucrative postings became obvious as soon as the position was relinquished. One could see the importance flying out of the windows.

So it finally began to dawn upon me that it was only dedicated selfless public service, which left behind an everlasting aroma and gave permanent dividends. Anything short of that was just opportunism. People will flatter you, use you, while you hold clout and then abuse and conveniently forget about you, once you lose the clout. People can go to any extent to polish people's egos but only a fool gets taken in by this tom- foolery. I was obviously one such fool.

Now I realise and repent the hollowness of the life that I had led. But I got lucky earlier then some of the other unlucky souls.

After a few years of restlessness, I realised I had trodden the wrong path. And then I started looking for 'meanings' in life. Those which I had casually discarded now seemed to be the only 'meaningful' milestones in the journey of my life. I knew now that truth and humility, the ability to forgive alone strengthened the purpose of one's life.

I sink with shame when I recall how I had misappropriated peoples' resources, how I had often humiliated and persecuted others.

One realises the importance of a given distance only when one is close to the finishing line. That is where one's potential is finally realised. But good runners are aware of this fact at the start and keep the necessary calculations in mind before setting their pace. Those who run without a purpose may win the race like the mice but remain rats in deed. Whenever the bitter memories of my ill deeds bother me, I turn to the Supreme Being who guides me to perform some meaningful acts. Perhaps that may help erase some of those ill deeds I have committed through the course of my life.

Policing is a profession that entails deeds which cannot be proclaimed as pure and often not at all fair. Many have suffered the onslaught of our canes even though they may have been innocent spectators during violent communal outbursts. Where is the time to verify who is innocent and who is not! I remember an incident where a very senior professor was lathi charged by my cops in my presence. Later, when he met me in a social function, he broke down. Probably, the brunt of the humiliations that he had borne had finally spilled over. How could I explain to the suffering, hurt soul that the husk too unfortunately gets ground along with the grain? I apologized.

Similarly, people often get implicated falsely during investigations. I can recall two such incidents. When the public outcry and media pressure increased and as the crime could not be successfully worked out, we decided to go in for a general combing of the concerned areas. It goes without saying that many atrocities are a by-product of such a drive. A rogue thrashed, is a job well done but if in the bargain an innocent man is demeaned, that niggles the conscience.

Now that such memories keep surfacing, it perturbs me and my conscience to no end. There was a time when running aimlessly or following the rat race, nothing bothered me. But now those ignonimous acts of mine drill holes in my injured heart. The wounds continue to bleed.

I can only beg for forgiveness and look forward to helping myself to off load the burden my heart carries.

I have been making an untiring effort to pen down my own obituary for the last twelve years, but to no avail. I have failed miserably in all my efforts. What can

I possibly write? Is there any side of me, that is praiseworthy? It is easier to extol others. But, here I am my own mission where the reflections of my past misdeeds boomerang. They are beaming out of my present reflection. I cannot declare the black as white. I desperately need to justify my acts but how?

After I joined the police, every dead body was a reminder to me of my prime duty and the motto of my service. Gradually, they stopped to make an impact. Sensitivities began to vanish. We talked of the dead statistically and rejoiced in the killings. We enthralled in the numbers, "Ten murders last month, only eight this month". That is life's irony. No one was bothered why even a single life was lost, forget that so many were lost.

We had even learnt the art of 'effective' reportings. And I must confess that I too had been instrumental in the magic of the numbers. I used this technique often either to pulverize my enemies or to befool my opponents. The thought now gnaws at my intestines. How could I? What was the dire need to? Why did I live life piecemeal? I today feel inadequate. A stunted man who deserves to be condemned and shunted to the periphery of life's main battle ground.

"O Anand! The traveller has finally traversed the entire length of his life's journey. The sun has set. The night is upon you, what now?" My body weakens, refusing to support me any further. I shall soon be bedridden, a vegetable and become part of that very 'game of statistics' – a mere number!

A golden opportunity had knocked at my door. I could have provided relief to many but I had chosen instead to inflict fresh wounds. I was offered the opportunity to embalm their souls with a humane touch.

Instead I pricked their self respect and the right of being a human being. They approached me with fresh hope. But my ego prevented me from lending them a sympathetic ear. I suffered from the malaise of insensitivity and a lack of humility. I could not bow down and entertain their imploring, mercy calls. I thrived on a self generated false ego. My heels carried me along strutting the glimmering stars that adorned my shallow undeserving shoulders. I preened over the forced salutes of the sentries around me. Like the bullock that moves round and round the traditional oil press with its eyes shut and then when it opens its eyes, it discovers it hasn't moved an inch, so had been my plight.

I had to my credit a gallantry medal and medals for meritorious and distinguished services. I was also awarded the commendation certificates that adorn the walls of my living room even today. This world would adjudge me a successful officer with so much to my credit. But here when I attempt to pen down the so called positives I feel the suffocation in my gut set in. My hands refuse and turn lifeless. My mind refuses to even fleetingly nurture the thought, let alone live it. I am incapable of awarding any 'certificate' to myself!

When I turn in after a day's grind, even sleep elludes me. The walls of my room come alive. They depict gory mutilated faces, faces of my past. Then they gradually assume the shape of an eagle, the bird of prey, and it begins to eat away at my intestines, may be this is how I shall eventually reach a state of self actualisation and then I will come prepared to say to my Lord the Almighty "Accept me now, take me in your fold, Divine Spirit!

* * *

ADDENDUM

'Story telling' is one of the most popular ways of communication, of getting across the thoughts that picturise reality in a more subtle manner. It also provides more manoeuvrability so as to fit in the emotions, along with the physical environment, such that a cognitive background is effectively drawn for a strong interface.

The various facets of insurgency in Assam, the plight of the local populace, the woes of the victims of insurgency and political exploitations have been laid bare through the lens of the security forces.

Various 'conflict dimensions' can be viewed in terms of –

- Historical demographic invasions
- Inter-tribal rivalries
- Economic migration
- Multi-ethnic political aspirations

- Trans border under currents
- Low cost – high impact terrorism
- Fracturing of the larger social fabric

The earlier settlers in Assam are believed to be related to the Sino-Tibetian ethnic group (ancestors of the present title of the Bodos) who settled down in the vast Brahmaputra plain. Other early settlers include groups such as the Dimasa-Kacharis and Koch-Rajbonsshies. Significant migration then subsequently flowed from the Indian mainland consequent to the introduction of the Brahmanical religious ideas. The demographic and territorial structure of Assam experienced substantive change with the arrival of the Ahoms from the Chinese regions in the eleventh century A.D. While the Brahmanical elements of the Assamese got coopted with the new Ahom political and cultural structure but in the bargain, the older ethnic groups got increasingly marginalised. The demographic panorama further underwent a paradigm shift with the advent of the British. It will not be out of place to pen down the observation that much of the present problems in Assam have been the direct outcome of the British Colonial interest. Fresh waves of immigration during the period flowed into the segments of tea-cultivation where the Adivasis were inducted, administrative arena where Bengalis, predominantly Hindu, remained the pivot and cultivators from East Bengal came to occupy the vast fertile Brahmaputra valley. Demographic tensions, that were already aggravated by the end of the British rule, further got a boost in the form of the refugee influx from East Pakistan (now Bangladesh) in the post partition scenario. Illegal immigration from Bangladesh continued unabated even later on posing a serious challenge to the demographic equation.

All these sub optimal confluences finally made a dent in the form of a political marginalisation of the ethnic Assamese. A demand for the ouster of 'foreigners' gradually started to echo, once the Hindu caste Assamese started to react. The tensions felt by the minority tribal groups of the Bodos, Kacharies and Dimasas sought their manifestation in the form of violent acts. Each such group aimed to create a safe heaven for its own tribe. Inter-tribal rivalries, thus, also flourished on this fractured zone.

In fact, it will not be wrong to look at the migrations in terms of 'economic' attraction. Vast, fertile and uncultivated tracks, commercial cultivation based on labour intensive practices and requirements of educated manpower for running a British administrative set up, all combined together to form fuelling factors for the purpose.

Over a period of time, political aspirations exclusively led to decentralised formats of conflicts demanding an autonomous rule by different ethnic groups. The ethnic polarisation witnessed marginalisation of smaller groups over a period of time adding further discontiguities to the conflict grid. The various players of the game have been working at cross purpose, at times taking a segmental view and nurturing their own interests. The role of the stakeholders, thus, has to be scanned to see the emerging formats of conflicts and plausible solution domains –

- Political elite
- Power brokers and arbitrators
- Ethnocentric insurgent groups (demanding autonomy with different vested interests)

- Insurgent leaders (hybernating abroad with ulterior motives).
- Trans border agencies (guiding the flow of insurgency creating surrogate bases)
- Cultural ambassadors
- Social elite and intellectuals
- Frontal organisations and NGOs
- General governmental agencies
- Security forces
- Media and perception managers
- Legal watch dogs

It appears that the traditional political elite have been co-opted into the mainstream to some extent. The fringe players, however, have been generating a source of worry with divergent political ideologies looming large in the existing scenario. Susceptibility of such fringe elements to manipulation by vested interests has a beaming effect. Multiplicity of ethnic groups makes the situation for the various stake holders rather tough when it comes to balancing mutual interests. This only suggests that real solution vectors can be located in the grid where efforts are being made to get these diverse ethnic groups into the main political mainstream, may be through gradual demarcation of territorial jurisdiction, so as to set in the process in some form or the other. When relationships mature over a period of time due to socio-cultural or economic holicism, may be the demarcations convulge into some united formats. Hence, the process of negotiated settlement still makes sense.

Amidst such a situation, the emergence of political power brokers and arbitrators has a deep significance. They not only aid in starting peace processes but also provide a saving face to the affected groups. By proving the sincerity of intentions and projecting the ethnocentric grievances as the focal issue of negotiation, such peripheral violent groups may be brought within the peace grid, keeping the functional issues in close brackets and repeatedly harping on their growth avenues.

However, the peace initiatives receive a set back when the insurgent groups, based abroad, work at creating terror and garnering propoganda through local disgruntled elements. The ideological disillusionment of the public, amidst such a situation, provides a winning platform for the peace makers, if rightly converted into an opportunity.

The conflict in this zone, having prolonged for decades and given ample opportunities to various operatives within and around the region, has attained further complexities with the arrival of motivated terror modules through Jehadi outfits and agencies nurturing such outfits for ulterior strategic interests in the region. Thus, trans border agencies have added a new facet to the conflict and has become a package of global terror.

Security agencies alone cannot make a dent in such a situation. There is a need for perception management through cultural ambassadors, non governmental bodies and the social elite. In the process, the frontal organisations nurtured by the conflict groups too need to be properly countered and neutralised. The developmental agencies also need to expedite their performance to generate economic interdependence and well neturalised 'quality life'. Combined with various psychological operations, the public response to the disgruntled elements would definitely change. After all, nothing can survive without public support.

Conflict resolution strategies involve multi-faceted interventions–

- Negotiations and ceasefire talks
- Surrenders and diversion to National mainstream
- Armed response for wiping out the subvertors
- Diplomatic efforts to control trans border assistance
- Democratic activation for inroad to political power
- Socio-cultural interventions
- Balancing economic stakes
- Managing undercurrents
- Undertaking psychological operations

Negotiations and ceasefire arrangements, though formed effective conflict resolution strategy in case of Bodos in the beginning, finally leading to formation and autonomous Bodo council; the failure of negotiation initiatives between Government of India and ULFA has remained a cause of concern. Consequently, the peace negotiations arrived at with other ethnic groups are also oscillating without any final outcome as they are being guided by a wrong demonstration effect by the ULFA and the covert use of their cadres by the latter for various subversive acts. The central leadership, particularly those heading military segments, need to be tackled well.

While the organisational level initiatives continue, efforts have also been made to get back individual cadres to the national mainstream through attractive packages under surrender and resettlement policies. Here, the role played by perception managers in the system and functional intermediaries also becomes important. Though instances are there, which indicate siphoning of the funds and other benefits through fake surrenders, yet strategically, the given option remains a potent source of thinning down the base of insurgent groups and rechannelising the misdirected youth. The concern of security agencies towards recycling of such surrenderees may be relevant to an extent but not valid to the point of renunciating this option. In addition to the armed response in the low intensity war zones by security forces, they remain stable options as no conflict can go on for ever, much less in the sphere where we have to deal with our own people who have taken up arms due to some mismatch or the other. It is definitely different than dealing with the enemy across the border.

Diplomatic efforts have paid results from time to time with ULFA making its bases in Bhutan. The operations launched by the Royal Forces along with Indian contingents few years ago did pay dividends. Similar diplomatic efforts are called for in Bangladesh and Myanmar as the target groups reportedly have spread their wings there now, in order to create a base and their launching pads. The task may be different due to historical and strategic intricacies, as known generally to all of us, but the option cannot be closed.

Another important conflict resolution strategy is to strengthen democratic institutions at the grass root level, say panchayats or the tribal bodies, such that the environment of self governance dissuades the external forces to misdirect the people for any revolt. Socio-cultural initiatives for perception management are also equally crucial. One thing we should not undermine is the presence of various undercurrents which decide the real course of the conflicts. Hence, the systems have to be built in to sense these flows. Overt activities may be deceptive. Hence, role of the intelligence agencies becomes important to guide executive cadres of the government in deciding upon various strategic interventions. The psychological operations have, therefore, to be carried out with persistence and with 'hidden hands' to generate positive cognitions.

All wars finally end up in peace, but till a final state of peace is achieved we cannot relax our security options. A fine balancing of the given options is the real art at which the managers of peace at the apex level have to be adept at. However, I would like to emphasise on the doctrine of counter insurgency operations in a nutshell before ending this book.

ESSENTIALS OF COUNTER INSURGENCY DOCTRINE

Insurgencies have been finding their ways owing to fractured aspirations of various demographic segments. Dissemination leading to stratification of various degrees, coupled with socio-economic exploitation, vitiates the environment to the extent that people take to armed rebellion with an aim to seek right of self-determination and an autonomous political set up. Susceptibility of such groups to manipulation by various vested interests further adds a spectrum of disillusionment where virtual grievances eclipse the 'reality'. There are then no linear solutions. The counter insurgency (C.I) measures under such situations call for system synergies of a different order. It may take volumes to deal with various facets of a viable C.I. approach. However, we cannot miss the basic essentials:

- *The basic policy of the authorities ought to aim at bringing the people back to the mainstream through integrated effort and not 'armed response' alone. It is not a war against the enemy. It calls for an approach where misdirected potentials have to be channelised for constructive framework, simultaneously mitigating the factors responsible for disenchantment.*

- *Well configured security forces in terms of skills, equipments, motivation and overall nurturing ought to be deployed to tactfully deal with the issue. Common masses are used by the masterminds of insurgency to operationalise the plans. Security forces also, more often than not, come in contact with such captive groups who are largely mere 'puppets'. Hence, well directed plans, zeroing down on the main players, have to form a part of the security forces' strategy. It has to be a people friendly professional force not guided by numbers alone in terms of statistical achievements.*

- *Effective security grids need to be evolved, having studied the geographical and demographic intricacies. The core areas have to be identified and swept clean by plugging the escape routes.*

- *Security linked development has to be the main approach so that 'push' factors are also neutralised and people get a conducive environment for self development as well as a secure existence.*

- *Intelligence generation has to be given top priority for effective weeding out of the hard core criminal elements. In fact, intelligence networks provide an opportunity to the responsible citizens to join the fight against insurgency by providing timely inputs to the security forces. Though "professional sources" have also strongly surfaced in this field owing to the peculiarity of the task while the 'ulterior vectors' play heavily on the security matrix.*
- *However, one thing which cannot be undermined is the 'humane' approach within the violent responses of counter insurgency operations. The basic dignity of the human being has to be maintained with a minimum use of force and without collateral damages. The response of the security forces moulds the public cognitions.*
- *Security forces should also develop effective public interface through community action programmes, remove the blockades and build the bridges of confidence through generation of civic facilities which can improve the quality of life of the insurgency ridden populace.*
- *Systems should also be built for the honourable surrender of the misguided youth and other elements who wish to return to the mainstream. The cogent rehabilitation packages should be evolved providing avenues for the growth of skills and economic sustenance for a peaceful, respectable existence.*
- *Negotiation and peace processes ought to be continued through intervention of the diplomatic, political or socio-cultural elite trying to arrive at a win-win situation for the insurgency laden groups as well as*

the government. The various formats that evolve over a period of time do, however, provide workable solutions with given checks and balances.

- *Much attention has to be paid to the under currents as various stake holders tend to play their own games and create a hidden matrix which involve far more different vectors than what is apparent. Hence, superficial solutions would tend to fail and wash away public confidence in the authorities if hidden vectors are not duly taken cognisance of. What we need is the capacity to observe and absorb.*
- *Last, but not the least, what is of critical import should not be missed. This is as important as any other operation against the armed rebellion. The efficacy of 'perception management' has to be judged at every moment and the efforts be renewed. It could be anything from media handling to the handling of frontal organisations or the NGOs. Added to the spectrum of such efforts are the psychological operations covertly launched through nurtured support groups and the third party interventions under the different garbs.*

I would also submit that the views expressed here are personal and nothing amounts to an official stand, as such, on any matter.

I would like to end this culminating write up with the following quote :

"Good leaders show greater than average willingness to take risks and engage in unconventional actions to attain their goals."

- the author

* * *

INDEX

☆ ☆ ☆

ISBN
97881704933100